THE CLAIBORNE INSTITUTE

By
George L. Hoffman

PUBLISH AMERICA

PublishAmerica

Baltimore

First printing

ISBN: 1-59129-528-9
PUBLISHED BY PUBLISHAMERICA BOOK
PUBLISHERS
www.publishamerica.com
Baltimore

Printed in the United States of America

~ To my sister, Jean, and the many other good people to whom bad things have happened ~

Foreword

This is a work of fiction inspired by the ongoing question in the minds of many humans who ask, "Why do bad things happen to good people?" The only answers I have heard or read thus far have been nebulous platitudes that create much smoke and provide little light. Though I have tried to eliminate much of the smoke, some readers of this novel are expected to complain about the light I have tried to generate. Perhaps it will be too revealing for some, not revealing enough for others. To those critics I must say, "Light your own lamps, create your own smoke!"

~ The Author

INTRODUCTION

In 1970, at age fifty-five, John Claiborne went home to the Canadian River country of his birth. But it wasn't to that huge lovely land on the States' northern border to which he went. It was, rather, to a place unknown to the real Canadians and, perhaps, equally unknown to the majority of those inhabitants of the states themselves. How the twin rivers came to bear their names is a mystery since they in no way can be remotely associated with the country of Canada. Even John Claiborne did not know the origin of the two rivers' names.

As fraternal twins, the North and South Canadian Rivers travel similar routes from the same highlands of Northeastern New Mexico. But they seem less like rivers and more like winding expanses of sand with thin silver threads of water seeking their uncertain way to the distant Arkansas. When he first pointed the South Canadian River out to the young wife whom he was taking home to meet his parents in 1938, she had squinted through the car window and asked, "River? What river?"

"I am embarrassed to call it a river," he had said. "It's those two lines of trees and the sandy flat between them. You'll have to look hard to find the water this time of year."

And she had smiled at his discomfort and snickered, "Well, it's really a river of sand, isn't it?" And, reverting back to her high school Spanish, she shook her head knowingly and joked, "That's what I would call it, Arena Del Rio!"

"It's a much prettier name than South Canadian," John Claiborne admitted, "but the natives wouldn't like it. They are a hard-nosed lot who don't like outsiders changing things."

She had snuggled up close to his side and murmured, "I hope I won't give them reasons to feel that I am an outsider, John. I want to be family. I want them to love me as I love you. I'll never do anything to make them consider me differently."

"I know you won't," he had assured her. "I wouldn't have married you if I had thought that."

And, after a thirty-two year storybook marriage, he knew how correct he had been. She had never in any way indicated anything but pride and admiration for his Oklahoma background. John Steinbeck's Okie label, which had insinuated itself into the California vernacular, infuriated her, and she never hesitated to rebuff those who dared to use it in her presence. She was fiercely proud of her husband.

And she should be. By age forty, he had taken charge of her family's construction business and built it into one of the most successful on the West Coast. After her father's death, they had taken it over, streamlined it for efficiency, and branched out to build shopping centers, apartment complexes, and highways. When the wartime economy slowed in Southern California, they, with their only son, Frank, as a junior partner, moved their entire operation to Las Vegas.

The smell of money with the rapid rise of the gambling and entertainment industry was a powerful incentive to the building industries as well, and the Claiborne Construction Corporation prospered. But the eastern mobs also smelled the money, and the CCC Corporation, as it became known, soon found itself pressured to be less competitive in making bids for the lucrative contracts. CCC refused. The subtle suggestions became demands, and the demands became threats. Unused to such strong-arm practices, John Claiborne became worried and conciliatory. But son Frank refused to negotiate and went to the authorities. That news traveled quickly on the underground pipeline, and Frank turned up missing the next day. His body was found by a fisherman a week later floating in the waters of Lake Mead. He left his young widow, their five year old son, and two peace loving, law abiding parents devastated.

The Federal Bureau of Investigation got involved, and after months of undercover work, it arrested two suspects. One chose to testify in exchange for a more lenient sentence. Both went to prison. But the awful blow had been struck and with terrible consequences. Angela, the devout young widow, tearfully declared that she could no longer live to rear her young son in such a sinful environment. She returned to her own roots.

She had met Frank at a family gathering in El Reno, Oklahoma several years earlier when his parents had returned there to attend a family reunion. Through in-laws unrelated to the Claiborne family, her path had crossed that of the handsome young man from California. An intensive courtship followed, and the two were married later that winter.

For six years, she found herself living in the strange, glitzy world of Las Vegas. She, with her strict Baptist upbringing, felt lost and confused, but her devotion to her husband helped her to endure her unhappiness until he was no longer a reason to endure it. "I will take my son back to El Reno where some semblance of decency exists," she vowed. "I will not raise my son in this sinful city!" With her dead husband's ample life insurance proceeds, she returned to her roots.

It was prod enough for the grieving parents of Frank Claiborne. They decided it was time to explore their own options.

"I want to go home," John said.

"I do, too," agreed Meg, "but the home I once knew no longer exists. The big house with its orange groves where I grew up in Pomona has been replaced with apartment complexes. We built them there, remember?"

"I remember," John muttered. "The only place I know that hasn't changed much is where I grew up. It remains uncluttered with the trappings of this frantic world. It is still a place of times past."

"Like in the musical, where the wind blows free across the plains?" his wife asked.

"It does that, all right," he agreed, "and you would soon get tired of that. Oklahoma isn't known for having a lovely climate."

"Neither is Las Vegas. Without the glitz and hoopla, it would be sagebrush and sand."

"Do you want to leave here, Meg?"

"Oklahoma sounds much better than this, John. You have lived in my world for thirty years. I am willing to try yours for the next thirty. Besides the only family we have is there. Mine has gotten swallowed up in the megalopolis of Los Angeles, and I have lost touch with everyone. With Frank gone, I don't have a family anymore except yours. If that is where your heart is, it's where mine will be."

"You mustn't forget Angela and our grandson," her husband chided. "They are family, too."

"I'm not so sure, John. Angela never embraced us as family like I embraced yours. She has regarded us more as aliens who happened to birth her husband. I don't believe we have ever been family to her."

John sniffed and muttered, "You know why, don't you, Meg? We don't fit her Baptist image of good God fearing Christians!"

"I know," agreed Meg. "Some religion is to be expected in most people, but like anything else, it can be too much of a good thing when they expect everyone to believe the same way they do."

"Frank had some bad times trying to live up to her expectations," John said, shaking his head sadly. "She was all the time giving him Hell for working on Sunday instead of going to church with her."

"Those are pretty strong words, John!"

"They aren't mine," he said defensively. "They were Frank's. He said more than once that he was caught between two Gods, business and religion. I guess he couldn't quite choose between the two. I know that he loved her and all that, but if two people were ever a miss-matched pair, it was those two. Maybe that's why he got a little reckless when he challenged the mob."

"You aren't blaming her, are you, John? She didn't have anything to do with that."

He looked sorrowfully at the floor and shook his head. "No, I am not. She was just reacting to her family's teachings as he was to his. The mistake was made when they married. They got blinded by their romantic notions of love and forgot to analyze the facts."

"That's passed," Meg murmured, "and nothing will bring Frank back. Now, we have to wonder about our grandson. We do have a grandson, John. We can't just shut him out of our lives."

"Yes, we do have a grandson," John agreed, "and if his mother will let us, we should try to be there for him if he needs and wants us. That is one more reason I want to go back."

"It's reason enough," Meg said.

Six months later, with their extensive holdings turned into company stocks and cash assets, they went home to Oklahoma.

Chapter 1

In the spring of 1970, John and Meg Claiborne parked their big pickup truck and travel trailer next to the large cedar tree that John had known as a small boy. It had been a transplant from a grove near the edge of the river breaks. On his sixth birthday in 1921, his father and he had selected it to be a memorial tree to be planted in honor of his first day of school. Each year thereafter, the ritual had continued, and that tree was now the largest and most beautiful of a long line of trees stretching east to west along the southern border of the family homestead. With the sixteenth tree, the ritual had ceased. That fall, John had begun the last year of his civil engineering studies at the state college in Stillwater.

"This grove will be your memorial," his father had said. "Come back to it as often as you can."

And John had. Each fall when the heat of August was past, he and Meg had returned to spend part of their vacation time in the big farmhouse that his father had built in 1928. That year had been the last of the good years, for the hard times of drought and depression had followed. But his family had endured, and John had managed to eke out a college career with mortgage money on the family farms. When he returned in 1938, he brought with him a new bride and money enough to pay off the mortgages. He would in subsequent years buy the family holdings where his parents were content to spend their last years. More land was bought as it became available, and the memorial grove of big cedars then marked the old homestead as the center quarter section of six others clustered along the ridge over looking the river. The other old farmsteads had been stripped of their houses and out buildings, and John and Meg Claiborne were returning to a world completely opposite from Los Angeles and Las Vegas. They were returning to solitude.

"It is so quiet," Meg said that evening.

"No traffic, no sirens," John murmured. "But there are sounds. You have to listen for them. I heard a bobwhite quail somewhere beyond the old house when we first stopped. At dusk, the coyotes will be tuning up, and the mocking birds will start their all night serenades. We might even hear the gobble of a tom turkey. I saw tracks in the road dust as we came in."

"I think I will like it, John," his wife whispered, as if afraid to taint the silence, "but give me time. My ears aren't used to hearing this kind of silence."

"We will take time," John assured her. "If it doesn't work out, we can always move to some place more suitable to your needs."

"And what of your needs, John?" Meg asked. "What about the town for retired Oklahoma natives you have always dreamed of building? I know you. You are too young to hole up in some maze of frenzied people. I am too, but I need some fellow humans around me. When we get things organized and your town is built, we will have the best of both worlds. I believe that. I will adjust!"

"Let's begin adjusting now," her husband said softly. "The sun will be going down soon, and we need to see that. Then the stars will be coming out, and we will see the sky as humans were meant to see it—a panorama of stars and constellations, with the Milky Way stretching all the way from horizon to horizon. I am home, Meg, and I hope you are, too!"

Together, they walked through the lengthening shadows along the edges of a field of young wheat. "We will build our town here," he said. He pointed toward the river with its silver ribbon of water nourished by the melting snows from the headlands in New Mexico. "Here, and on the ridges lying between the gullies and creeks leading to the river where the lots cannot be squeezed into tight little squares that smother each other, we will build a new town. People need room below as well as open skies above. They need space between themselves and their neighbors. Otherwise, they become ants and termites, and begin to behave like them."

"That will cost a lot of money," Meg suggested.

"Living anywhere costs money," John replied, "especially when land values are like they are on the West Coast. But here, the costs will be largely because of the necessary roadways, water, electric power, and sewers."

"How much per lot?" Meg asked.

"Three thousand, I would guess for a quarter acre lot."

"And a house, such as a three bedroom ranch of medium size?"

"Ten to fifteen thousand, maybe. Of, course that's another guess."

"We can't afford to guess, John," chided Meg.

"Right, Meg! That will be your job. You are good at breaking down costs. While I am getting surveys done, you can be calculating those costs. By fall, we will have a pretty good idea if this is a realistic project."

"Your figures would make each house and lot cost about eighteen to twenty-one thousand," Meg mused. "That would be a lot less than the same property in Los Angeles."

"And on a much larger lot than in LA!"

"Will there be buyers who are willing to live in this kind of climate and isolation?"

John took a deep breath and thought a moment. "Well," he said, "I think we can find plenty of retired people on the West Coast who will be glad to trade their rat's maze for what we could supply here. Ex-Oklahomans alone are surely pining for their old homeland. Not all, maybe, but enough that a bit of advertising would create the urge to investigate what we have. For those who have been squeezed into tiny parcels, space sells over climate. And a quarter acre with open skies and far horizons can be appealing. I am counting on that."

"When could we start this Utopia which you have planned?"

"If we get started immediately, we should know by next fall. I will have ads in most of the big papers out west before then and articles in the local papers as soon as next week. We can stir up a lot of interest locally which should be useful. Not much is happening here, and the notion that a new modern town is to be built on the banks of the Canadian River will create a shockwave through this entire area."

"Will it blow our cover and send prices up?"

"We have the land, so we will have no problem there. And building costs will be controlled by normal factors of competition and demand."

"You've gotten my attention," Meg said. "I was afraid that I would wither up and die for lack of something to do. Now, it sounds as if we may have our old operation back. Let's get started!"

"But we mustn't forget our grandson," he reminded her. "We need to make his mother realize how important he is to us."

"Yes," Meg agreed, "we will go to El Reno before we do anything else. We will go tomorrow."

Chapter 2

Angela Watts had always been something of an enigma to her peers. She did not meet the expectations usually reserved for an unusually pretty child of impeccable tastes and behavior. Perhaps, the confusing environment of her childhood was the cause, for it was a time unsettled by world war and its aftermath. Family disruptions and readjustment to peacetime living were not always conducive to lasting relationships. Many children of those families on the move did not have the duration of years to become intimately acquainted with their peers and to make bosom friends.

In the space of a dozen years, Angela had endured the loss of her father in that war and the discontent of her young widowed mother, striving to rationalize her young husband's desire to volunteer to fight in a war in which he was to become a casualty. Returning to the home of the old grandmother in El Reno, Oklahoma when Angela was ten years of age would later give a symbolic stability to their lives. There, in a matriarchal home devoid of male figures, Angela was to spend her adolescent years.

But the twig had been bent and so grew the tree. The young girl had heard the older women's stories of failed relationships with their male counterparts, and their deep-rooted suspicions regarding the masculine mystique were to shape her in many ways.

But it was in her high school years that the enigma became most evident. As she matured into a strikingly beautiful blond, the expected vanity and giddy behavior, often accompanying such rare beauty, were not present. She remained cool and aloof to those who would be her friends, and disdainful of the fawning young males who dared to be her admirers. Angela Watts was indeed strangely different! For lack of better explanations, she was labeled a conceited, egotistical snob.

That was not true, of course, for she had been shaped by environmental and spiritual factors rather that physical ones. Some of her critics believed that Angela was a reincarnation of the original Eve. She walked in her shadow, and even she believed that Eve's original sin might be her curse, as it seemed to be for so many other women struggling to live in a male world. "I will not succumb to their lust and evil ways!" she vowed.

Her world outside the one of books and classrooms became that of her grandmother and mother. Deeply religious, they lived according to the dictates of their Bible and the admonitions of their pastor. And Angela followed their example.

But, with her developing womanhood, all of the worldly temptations of the flesh came to bedevil her, and she recognized them for what she believed them to be. Eve's sin had come to haunt her. Satan, so often in the presence of humans, was in pursuit of her. She willed herself to be strong, and, in spite of the erotic impulses she often experienced in the presence of healthy young males, she prevailed. She refused to let herself become intimately involved with young men, and she chose not to attend school parties and the school proms. The thought of dancing in close contact with one of the opposite sex both titillated and frightened her, and she understood her church's aversion to such behavior.

At eighteen, the number of social contacts with hopeful young men had been limited to those few in the cloistered affairs of her church. She sang in the church choir, served on youth committees, and often helped with religious programs. "I will know a man in the Biblical sense only with the sanctity of marriage," she promised herself. Then, in her eighteenth year, the handsome young man from California came into her life.

It was a random meeting. A family reunion involving strangers in the local park was not in her plans. She didn't even know the family, but a friend from the church had invited her to go to meet some interesting relatives from California. It was Saturday, the weather was favorable, and life had grown a bit humdrum. Angela decided to go. On such random decisions the events of a lifetime are often determined. It was so for Angela Watts.

The friend had been a daughter of the family hosting the reunion, and their regular church attendance and participation at church affairs gave them and their guests some credibility as good Christian people. Angela was quick to assume that Frank Claiborne was of that favored tribe. He was quiet, confident, and modest. He was also exceedingly handsome and masculine. Angela fell, and she fell hard.

Frank was making his own assumptions. Fresh from the glamour capitals of the post-war world, he saw her startling beauty as rivaling that of the many aspiring starlets in Hollywood. He also saw her modesty and quiet demeanor as signs that she was the old fashioned kind of girl he wanted for a wife. In subsequent visits to Oklahoma, he wooed her with a passion that left her gasping for breath, while she, at the same time, was defending her chastity with a determination that convinced him of her high moral purpose. They married, and when the passions of their honeymoon were finally sated, they began to learn their real differences. His world was that of corporate business. Hers was religion. Both worlds were real and valid, but difficult to mix.

Angela was a no-nonsense Christian. She attended church regularly and depended on it for its scriptural lessons. She could not understand Frank's disinterest. He tried to pacify her by going to church on a few occasions, but usually found reasons not to go. She had not known of his family's ambivalence toward religion and the lack of it in their lives. But she began to be suspicious of their disregard for spiritual values, and her suspicions soon turned to resentment for their neglect to teach their son Christian values. One way or another, her marriage was doomed to fail. And it did six years later with the death of Frank at the hands of mob hoodlums. She was left with a mixture of grief and relief. Both would follow her back to Oklahoma and harden her to the task of raising her son and sheltering him from the worldly influences that had shaped her husband. She was dismayed, eight months later, to learn that the elder Claibornes were also returning to Oklahoma, and she dreaded to think that they might in time want to insinuate themselves back into her son's life.

Bertha Watts, peering from a curtained window, saw the big pickup truck with its long travel trailer pull slowly onto the grassy shoulder. She saw the California license plate and gasped, "They are here, Angela! Are you going to invite them in?"

"I have to," was the reply to her mother. "Christian decency demands that." Angela Claiborne straightened her skirt and brushed back her hair as she watched the grandparents of her son study the surrounding area. Aware that their house carried no identifying street number, she stepped onto the big porch and went to meet them. She forced herself to be cordial. "You have found the right place," she called. "Please come in."

John Claiborne looked again at the surrounding grounds and nodded approvingly. "We weren't sure. You have a nice place, Angela. Nice and roomy."

"Nice and quiet, too," Angela agreed. "It's so different from the apartment in Las Vegas. Carol is very happy here."

Meg saw the tricycle parked in a porch corner and felt a small twinge. It was the Christmas present Frank has bought him when he was four. "He still has the tricycle, I see," she said. "I'll bet he enjoys that."

"Yes, he does," Angela sighed. "In Vegas, he had no place to ride it. Here he does. Please come in." She led them into the cool interior of the big house and introduced them to her mother and grandmother. They were coolly civil and restrained. Polite conversation followed.

John Claiborne looked at his watch. "I suppose that Carol is in school," he said. "We hadn't stopped to consider that. How is he doing?" He wanted to ask other questions but refrained. "Does he miss his father?" he wondered. "Does he miss us? Will he even remember us?"

Angela clasped and unclasped her hands. She smiled briefly and took a deep breath. "He's in first grade and doing very well," she said softly. "He loves school. Oh, I must tell you about what he did. He complained to me about his name. 'Carol is a girl's name!' he said, 'but if I leave out the O it will be a boy's name, Carl.' So now he goes by that name. I may let him do that, but I'm not sure, yet. It could cause problems later."

John grinned. "Very smart," he chuckled.

Meg raised her brows. "It could make problems for the future," she agreed. "All records like Social Security, passports, and the like will need to be keyed to his birth certificate. Maybe just adding an L would be better. That would turn it into a boy's name."

"Maybe," Angela said, and the conversation stalled.

John took a deep breath and looked at Meg. She raised her brows. "What time will Caroll be coming home?" she inquired. She emphasized the name to indicate her preference.

"About 3:00 o'clock," Angela replied, "but he has Bible school at the church right after that. Perhaps, you should come back some other time."

"When would be a good time?" Meg asked.

Angela looked at her mother, her eyebrows, asking the question. Her mother shrugged. After a long pause, she also shrugged. "Some Saturday afternoon would be best," she murmured and yawned.

"We are only twenty miles away," John suggested. "If we can have your phone number, we'll call first." He added the number to others in his wallet, rose, and stepped toward the door.

Meg got up and followed him out. Before closing the door she repeated her husband's words. "We will call first," she said. As they went down the walk, she muttered, "For a warm April day, that house was very chilly!"

"I would call it 'The Christian Freeze'," John growled. "If we are to keep in touch with our grandson, we will have to devise some clever strategies."

"Like what?" asked Meg..

"Like joining the opposition."

"Like joining their church?" Meg exclaimed.

"Something like that!"

"Oh, John! For Heaven's sake!"

"For ours, too, Meg. And little Carl's, I expect. Those women with their saintly notions will ruin that boy. I'll become one of their good Baptists, if I have to!"

"It might not be so bad," Meg said, as they drove away.

Chapter 3

For two weeks John and Meg were busy with the difficult and dirty work of making the old Claiborne house livable again. They cleaned the lower rooms of debris, they scoured, and they painted. Windows were repaired, sagging doors straightened, the roof patched. Linemen reconnected electric and telephone service, and plumbers reactivated the water pump and plumbing to the outside well. When new kitchen utilities were at last brought in and installed, they took a breather.

"This will be only temporary," he kept reminding his wife. "When you have decided where the new house should be and how you want it built, we will make it a priority."

"This will be just fine for now," Meg assured him. "When the time comes for a new house, I think I would like it just north of that first big cedar tree. That can come when the plans for the town are finalized. This old house has seen a lot of living and is capable of seeing some more. But when the real hot weather comes, we might want some air conditioning installed. Would that be possible?"

"No problem, Meg! I'll have window units for each room set in next week. But, for now, why don't we take a breather and call Angela. We need to see little Carl before he has time to forget who we are."

"Caroll," Meg said, emphasizing the two syllables. "Caroll, with two l's. We don't want to confuse the boy any more than he probably is."

John grunted. "He says that his name is Carl. If he prefers that name, I'll call him that."

"Maybe. But if Angela thinks that you like it, she may decide to keep the old name. If he had been born at Easter Time in place of Christmas Eve, I wonder if she would have named him 'Easter'!"

"Now, that sounds a little catty, Meg, and doesn't quite fit you,"

John chided. "Let's be positive and agree that Angela will do whatever is best for her son. Let's give her a call and set a time for us to drive over there. We could suggest taking them out for lunch and maybe a movie later. Couldn't we do that?"

Meg sighed. "You're right," she admitted. "I guess I'm just tired. Lunch and a movie would be a welcome change. I'll call and see if Saturday is okay. I need to do some shopping, too. We can go early and get that done first. But I'm not certain that we will have an invitation to come. What then?"

John frowned. "We need to go and do the shopping anyway," he reminded her. "And lunch and movie will be a welcome change from all this work. Give Angela a call first."

But Meg got only a busy signal for her efforts. Later attempts were more successful. An older unfamiliar voice said, "Hello."

"Hello," Meg responded. "Is this the Watts residence?

"Well, it is and it isn't," the voice said. "I am Emma Corbett, Bertha Watt's mother and Angela's grandmother. May I ask who is calling?"

"This is Meg Claiborne, and I wish to speak to Angela." A long pause interspersed with faint background voices followed. One was a child's. Some moments later, Grandma's voice returned. "Well," she said, "Angela isn't here right now. Could I have her call you back later?"

"Yes, I would appreciate that," Meg replied. She gave her their newly acquired phone number and waited for further confirmation that her call would be returned. When she heard the telling click of a phone being hung up, she replaced hers on its cradle and turned to John.

"Angela is supposed to call me back. But I won't be surprised if she doesn't. Her grandmother said she wasn't in. It seemed a bit long for her to become aware of that, and I could hear other voices in the background. One was a child's voice, and I heard it say 'Mama.' Oh, John, why is she doing this?" She looked as if she might cry.

"Do you think that Angela was there?"

"I'm sure that she was, John."

"And that she deliberately decided not to talk to you?"

"What else? Who was talking in the background? Why would I hear a child unless it was Caroll?"

John was solemn. He shrugged and muttered, "Maybe it was Bertha Watts, Angela's mother. Maybe Angela was out shopping and Carl was with his other grandmother."

"That is possible," Meg sighed, "but I think I heard the child say 'Mama'. We'll know if Angela does call us back."

"And if she doesn't?"

"We'll know that even good Baptists can tell untruths, John. What will we do then?"

John's face was grim. "We will go to church next Sunday morning," he said.

Throughout that afternoon and the next day they waited for Angela's' call. It never came, and they made their preparations to attend church services the following Sunday. They had not been to a Sunday service for a long time, and both were somewhat nervous. To allay their concerns, each dressed modestly in conservative attire that would not mark them as worldly transplants from sinful Nevada. They walked sedately behind the rank and file of other churchgoers and presented themselves to the handsome young assistant pastor who was greeting the steady stream of visitors at the wide church door. Each shook his hand in turn and entered the vestibule where a young woman was handing out programs. John saw her immediately. It was Angela, and John nudged Meg to alert her.

Busy with her task, Angela did not see her in-laws enter. The programs were in her hand, ready to be presented to the next visitors, before she had her first look at the middle-aged couple standing before her. She gasped and drew back. Momentarily speechless, she took a deep breath and swallowed.

"Oh, my!" she stammered. "What are you two doing here?"

"Strange that you should ask," John murmured. "We are here for the same reason all these others people are. I presume that your church does welcome visitors." He carefully concealed his amusement at her uneasiness and took a program. As he stepped away, he saw Meg accept a program and say softly, "Thank, you Angela." Then, together they permitted an usher to lead them to an empty pew.

Their entry was quiet and unremarkable to everyone except Angela. For her, it was so unnerving that she gave her remaining programs to a second woman and excused herself. She did not sing well in the choir that morning, and her eyes were purposely averted from the pew where Meg and John sat. For John, the whole episode left him feeling sad and disappointed, with a twinge of guilt for having caused such discomfort for another human being. And for Meg, it was a moment of sorrow for having failed to know the love of a daughter-in-law whom she had wanted so much to love and cherish. As she sat there quietly in the church pew with the hymns of devotion and love penetrating her being, she wondered if it was too late. And she wondered, too, what deep and abiding flaw in the human spirit was manifesting itself. How had she failed?

Her mind traveled back then to the seven years that she had known Angela. And she tried to picture their two lives, separate and impossible to combine into a close relationship. Hers had been a demanding one as the second-in-command of a vigorous corporation requiring much of her time. She had not wanted to neglect that role, and she had not wanted to intrude too much into the personal lives of her son and daughter-in-law. Perhaps she should have, for she now realized that after the initial honeymoon was over, when Frank had found it necessary to resume his place in the family business, Angela must have been very much lost and alone in the strange environment of Las Vegas.

All that the young woman had known was back in the quiet Oklahoma town of El Reno. Her support groups of family and church were there where her former days could be filled with the attention of many people. Las Vegas had almost none of that. Only the church was available to her, and it was so much more impersonal than the one she had left behind. Sunday worship was the one time when she could feel a small part the strange world in which she had found herself. And even during that special time, she had had no husband or family with whom to share it. A deep aversion for her new surroundings and the people in it had left her scarred.

John and I are of those people, Meg thought, *and now we are here in her presence, in her church congregation, threatening to upset her and her son's life! It is not surprising that she hopes that we will just go away!*

She let her eyes flit briefly over the rows of many pews filled with solemn and attentive people. She saw the elderly, the family groups, and the mixed groups of young singles. And she saw, as she hoped she would, the grandmother and mother of Angela, and the small boy in their care. She nudged her husband and made a subtle motion in their direction. "Caroll is there with his other grandmother," she whispered.

John smiled and nodded. Only his lips formed the words. "I know," he said.

They spent the balance of the service dividing their time listening to what the minister was saying and observing the quiet respectful demeanor of the small boy who was their only living heir to the future.

"We have fences to mend," John whispered, as he laid a twenty dollar bill in the collection plate.

"Yes," Meg murmured, "we have some redecorating to do. We will begin immediately!" She added a second bill to the offering and smiled to see the small flicker of surprise on the elder's face as he waited to take the plate.

Chapter 4

But the fences did not present themselves to be repaired, as John and Meg waited hopefully outside the church for Angela and her family to appear. When the last of the congregation had dribbled through the big doors, Angela and her family had yet to show themselves. "What shall we do now?" Meg asked.

John felt the last bit of his former remorse dwindle away. He grew angry. "I am going inside to see if they are still there," he growled.

Meg took him by the arm and pulled him back. "No, John, don't. That will only make the matter worse. We will probably create a scene and lose all chance of seeing our grandson again. We need a strategy to find why this happening."

"Like what, for instance?"

"Like coming back here on a regular basis and waiting this out. These people are good people. The minister is a good man. His sermon was all about family and brotherly love. 'Reach out,' he said, 'to the lonely and downtrodden. Seek out their needs and administer to them.' He said that, John. Surely, Angela heard it. She cannot ignore us forever. We will seek out her needs and let her know that we have needs, too."

"She has needs, all right! She is so mixed up that I dread what she may be doing to her son. Whatever you say, Meg. Let's go find lunch somewhere."

They called Angela that evening and got no answer. They called again the next morning. She answered the phone with a question. "Who is calling please?"

"This is Meg," was the reply. "We were sorry to miss you yesterday—" She heard the telephone click and the return of the dial

28

tone. She looked at John and muttered, "She hung up on me."

John scowled and shook his head in disbelief. "What in Heaven's name is the matter with that woman? Why can't she at least do us the courtesy of making known her reasons for avoiding us?"

"I think that she is afraid of us, John," Meg sighed. "For some reason she is paranoid about our presence here. She definitely does not want us in her life. What shall we do now?"

"We can surrender quietly to her wishes, or we can keep calling until she agrees to talk to us," John said.

"I will guess that her mother or grandmother will be picking up the phone from now on," Meg replied. "And they might give us some answers. The grandmother is our best bet, I think. She seems more friendly that the other two."

"Let me give it a try," John suggested. "I will wait until we've had breakfast. Maybe they will be off guard. What is the grandmother's name? I'll ask for her."

"Emma Corbett. She is the one I talked to last week. I gather from the way she responded to my questions that she might reveal what the problem is."

"Emma Corbett? I'll ask for her," John said through puckered lips.

An hour later, John dialed the Corbett number. "Hello," a voice said.

"May I speak to Mrs. Corbett, please?" John replied in his most casual voice.

"Mama, it's for you," the voice yelled. John heard the slow muffled approach of feet and the sound of a chair being dragged out as if it were to be sat in. "Hello," a second voice said, "This is Emma Corbett."

Again in his best casual voice John replied. "Mrs. Corbett, this is John Claiborne who came to your house a few days ago to visit Angela. Do you remember?" He paused and heard a long sigh from the other end of the line.

"Yes, I remember," Mrs. Corbett said softly. "I want to apologize for Angela's attitude. I promised your wife that I would have Angela return her call. I know now that she didn't, and I feel badly about that. I don't like to make promises that aren't kept. But I don't know what I can do about it."

"Perhaps you can tell me why Angela is so set on ignoring us. We aren't bad people trying to intrude into her life. We just want to have some kind of relationship with our grandson. Since the death of our son, Frank, he is all the family we have left. Can you tell me why Angela is so dead set against us?"

"That is for Angela to say, and she is standing right here. I'll insist that she talk to you." Then John heard her say in a quiet but firm aside, "Angela, this man deserves some answers! You get over here and talk to him."

The next voice was impatient and angry. "This is Angela! What do you want to know?"

"Angela, please tell us what we have done to cause your anger for us. We are not bad people. We have done the best that we could to take you into our family. How did we fail?"

The reply was quick and short. John could almost taste the bitterness in the young woman's voice. "You and Meg raised Frank to be what he was. You failed to give him the Christian childhood he needed and deserved. I loved Frank, and needed him. But he did not love me enough to be the husband I believed he would be. I don't blame Frank for that. I blame his parents, and I do not want them in my son's life creating another un-Christian man like his father."

John was stunned. He could barely manage a weak acknowledgment. "I see," he murmured. He waited for the telling sound of the other receiver being replaced on its cradle. When it did not come, he added, "Then you do not want us being a part of our grandson's life?"

"You have nothing to give him that I cannot give him," Angela said curtly. "And you should know that I have met another man who I shall marry soon—a God loving man, recently ordained to serve in our faith. I have no doubt that he will be the kind of father to my son that Frank could not have been."

John felt anger welling up within him. The words came out sharply. "And what about the mother of that son? Will she give him a balanced vision of the real world, or will she fill him with nothing but religious dogma and fantasy? I hope not, Angela."

"He will be the kind of man that God wants men to be," she vowed. "He will have no need for your Las Vegas mentality." The quick dull thud of the receiver on its cradle marked the end of the conversation.

He looked at the receiver in his hand. Stunned disbelief was on his face. "Oh, good God Almighty!" he muttered. Turning, he looked at Meg and shook his head. "The woman is a fanatic," he exclaimed. "She blames us for raising Frank to be ungodly." Then, almost word for word, he repeated what Angela had said. "She plans to marry again soon. Some young minister," he added. "We no longer have a grandson. He has been made a captive by religious zealots."

"I guessed as much," Meg said tearfully. "What can we do?"

"Not much, I'm afraid. Parents' rights come before grandparents' rights. If she wants us to butt out, we'll have to butt out and get on with our lives."

"And lose all connection with Caroll?"

"I think that's already happened. If she marries again, he will have a new father. He won't need us."

"Does that mean that we won't be going back to their church? I rather liked going yesterday."

"We can go again, Meg, if you want. But would you like to go there and face that kind of animosity? Would you want, every Sunday, to see our grandson kept as a stranger with no hope of knowing him as a grandson? I'm not sure that I would."

"It would be very awkward. Maybe we could find a different church."

"Maybe, we could," John said. "When we get this town project going, we'll give it a try." And his prolonged silence as he dressed for work told Meg that her gentle husband was still grieving for a son lost to evil men in Las Vegas and a grandson lost to an over zealous Christian woman in El Reno.

Chapter 5

Throughout that spring and summer, John and Meg put their grandson out of their minds and kept busy with the numerous preliminaries necessary for beginning the construction of their new town. Zoning restrictions were investigated and were found to be minimal and of little consequence. Urban sprawl was not a problem in that little corner of the world. County officials were more interested in new properties to be added to their tax base than in the finer considerations of how that property was to be built and administrated. They did ask about a water supply and sewage disposal, and when Meg outlined their plans for those, a tentative nod of approval was given. It soon became apparent that Canadian County officials believed such a project to be just a pipe dream of outsiders who could not possibly be aware of the unfavorable location and climate in which the retirement town was to be built. They smiled and quickly stamped the required forms and turned their attention toward more pressing matters. Meg moved on to other concerns.

She investigated the availability of utilities, schools, and medical facilities. She also took note of the area's labor force and construction firms. She even got estimates of various costs for street and septic disposal units. All of her findings were carefully organized into a set of facts and figures to be taken home where she and John could study them in great detail. Their previous experiences in California and Nevada gave them an expertise that could almost guarantee the most efficient and cost effective completion of their project.

"It looks good," John said late one afternoon as the heat of August was beginning to curl Meg's eyebrows into question marks. "If we can make sure that we will have people willing to live here, our project will be feasible."

"Is that a big 'if' or a little 'if'?" Meg asked. "I am age fifty-three, and the only time I have ever been so hot was the time we drove through Death Valley in July of 1955. That was before air conditioning in cars. Do you remember, John?"

"I remember," John chuckled. "And I remember how hot it used to get in this old house in the summers when I was just a kid. In August of 1934, it got so hot that we wrapped wet towels around our necks. My brothers and I finally jumped into the horse tank to cool off. The water was green and scummy, but damn, it felt good. We spent the rest of the day cleaning the crud and scum out and letting the windmill pump in clear cold water. The whole family later wound up there."

Meg's eyebrows wrinkled into a frown. "John, this is worse than Las Vegas! I don't know if anyone will ever respond to your California ads. Why would old retired people leave comfortable homes out there to move here?"

John looked at his wife of thirty-two years. His face was pained. "You hate it, don't you Meg? If you say the word, we'll give it up and move to Colorado where it's cool. We don't have to stay here. We don't have a grandson anymore, and we can live anywhere we want."

"You didn't answer my question," Meg scolded. "Why would retired people want to live here?"

John studied the old worn floor beneath his feet and took a deep breath. He looked at Meg and said solemnly, "Because home is where the heart is, and many of those people's hearts are not in Los Angeles or San Francisco or the other overpopulated places. Out there, they huddle like laboratory rats in their little corners, longing to find a way out of the maze. I believe that, Meg. I believe that this climate will seem secondary to those good folk if they know we have a place with space and clean, fresh air. My dream is to have a communal family of good people who want neighbors and friends around them, not strangers next door or across the street."

Meg looked at her husband through her tears, and the heat seemed less severe as she reached across to him and took his two hands in hers. "Oh, John," she whispered, "you are so wonderful! I still find myself in awe of you! I wonder how I was ever so lucky to get you and keep you all these years."

He grinned and chuckled softly. "One so wonderful as you deserves to have a man like me," he murmured. "She also deserves to be comfortable and happy. When you feel this place is not a place where you can be both comfortable and happy, we will leave it and find another."

"I am both comfortable and happy here, John. Only if, and when, we find that your town is not possible will I consider alternatives." She kissed him long and passionately, and whispered, "When the sun has gone down and the stars are out, we will take cooling baths in the horse tank. Then we will make love like we did that night in Death Valley. Do you remember, John?"

"I remember," he said. "The horse tank is clean and waiting."

When Meg went to the rural mailbox the next morning, she found four responses to John's California ads. All were from older persons displaced by the social changes of the great depression and the war years. Three were newly retired and clearly longing for a less urban environment. All had origins in Midwestern America and were seeking information. Meg sent personal letters to each with details of climate, possible costs, and the agenda for the development of the projected town.

But the fourth one was from two successful San Francisco realtors who were intrigued by such a daring venture as the brochures had described. They both had been born and reared in western Kansas where life had been hard and unpromising. Like thousands of others, the young newlyweds had migrated to California where prosperity was a golden lady with a silk purse. That lure and their own determination to succeed had paid them well. As a husband and wife team, they had been eminently successful and were nearing retirement. Contemplating a future of semi-boredom and anonymity, they considered a return to their own roots in Kansas to be a much better option. The slight difference in location was a small negative factor. The wish to be a part of a new project in their chosen field was a big positive one. Their letter was one of caution and quiet optimism. The Grayson Realty Agency was offering its services.

Meg and John were quick to see the new possibilities and responded immediately. They also sent letters of inquiry to state agencies in California for information concerning the status and past history of such a company. The replies were all positive with high marks for reliability and professionalism, and a new constant was factored into the project's formula. Grayson Realty was invited to be junior partners with their office as a base of operations for promoting interest and dispensing information.

"If they live up to their reputation, our big problem of recruiting prospective citizens of your town will be simplified," Meg said.

"My town?" John said with raised brows. "I want it to be your town, too, Meg! Every social enterprise like this needs a queen bee to keep the workers organized."

Meg smiled at her husband's moment of whimsy. "And to get rid of the drones?" she asked. "According to my expertise regarding queen bees, their workers are all modified females. That would make you a drone, John."

"Hmmnnn," he mused. "Leave off the 'bee' part. I think I would rather have you as just the queen of the operation, which you are of course—my queen of the soon-to-be town of Nirvana."

"Oh, John, not Nirvana! That smacks too much of Buddhism. Too many Christian people would be suspicious or downright negative. Take Angela, for instance, she and dozens like her would be enemies right on our doorstep, and what we do not need is those kind of enemies."

"Really? I didn't know where the term came from. It sounded rather nice and appropriate. Maybe Chisholm or some such name would be more fitting."

"Why Chisholm?"

"Because one branch of the old Chisholm cattle trail crossed the river just a mile from here, and since no town in Oklahoma is named that, I think it might add a little romantic interest. Too, anything of local lore would help make our project look more authentic."

Meg was thoughtful. After a few moments of deliberation, she nodded. "Yes," she agreed, "that would be more fitting. Then I could be Queen of the Chisholm Trail. If nothing better comes up, we'll name our town, Chisholm."

The town was no longer anonymous. It had an identity like a child conceived but still unborn. Its embryonic heart was already beating, and by the fall of that year, when Albert Grayson and his wife, Barbara, made their first appearance at the invitation of John and Meg, its future birth was almost a certainty.

The Graysons liked what they saw. They had been picked up the previous day at Oklahoma City's Will Rogers Airport by heir hosts and installed in a refurbished upstairs room of the old farmhouse. They proved to be as gracious and congenial as their hosts, and after a dinner of good home cooked food and an evening's exchange of background experiences, the two couples were friends.

"I like them," Meg said later that night as she and John were preparing for bed. "They seem so much like ourselves."

"Yes," John agreed. "Maybe they have the luxury of no longer feeling the need to prove themselves. I hope that by tomorrow when we show them the platted layout of Chisholm and the survey work we have done, they will give us some positive feed back. I'm even hoping that they might be influenced by our beautiful fall weather and want to become charter members of Chisholm."

"I think they would make first class citizens and neighbors," Meg sighed. "And, John, I do need that kind of social structure so very much."

"We both need that, Meg, and my instinct tells me that our town will attract those kinds of people—the kind who are looking for peace and serenity, warmth and security, and most of all the company and fellowship of caring friends and good neighbors. And I think they will want those things so much that they will overlook our extremes of climate. A fall day like we had today was impressive to the Graysons. I could tell it when they got off the plane, and I could tell it when Albert Grayson walked outside with me before we came up to bed."

"I suppose that you reminded him to look at the stars," Meg chided, as she stepped into her pajamas.

"I did, and he was astounded," John declared. "All he could say was, 'My, God! I had forgotten what the sky is supposes to look like!' And when he heard the horned owls talking from the big cedars above the house, he murmured, 'Oh, how wonderful!'"

"Do you think that he is hooked?"

"I hope so. We can really use him on our team." He yawned mightily, and went to sleep to dream of a Christmas Eve when a small boy's arms were about his neck and a teary-eyed face had sobbed, "Grampa, baby Jesus has to sleep in the manger with the animals!"

Chapter 6

"Your plans for this new town are more extensive and detailed than I had expected," Albert Grayson said the next morning, as he poured over the plats spread across the big dining table.

"And quite ambitious, too," his wife, Lenore, said with raised eyebrows. "Can such a town, with a proposed five hundred lots, spring full blown out of such a remote area with no industrial or commercial economy to sustain it?"

John was very thoughtful. He understood such skepticism. It had been present in nearly every project that he had masterminded in his thirty years of construction work out West. In every case, money had been the prime consideration—money to birth the project and money to nourish and keep it healthy as it aged and grew to maturity. The money to bring this new project to fruition was Claiborne money, carefully amassed in his and Meg's productive years. He was daring to risk some of that money now on an unproved dream that could die after those Claiborne assets were mostly exhausted. He squinted up at the skeptics and chose his words carefully.

"This is not a boom and bust enterprise," he said. "It will not depend on a growth factor with huge sums to drive an industrial complex and work force, and its product will not be material goods tied to an uncertain economy. It is to be, rather, an enterprise supplying amenities that I believe to be in short supply for a segment of our population with retirement incomes. Those incomes can fuel their demand for those amenities."

"You are implying," Harold Grayson said, with a degree of skepticism, "the old law of economics, the law of supply and demand?"

John nodded. "But, like any product, it must be made known and sought after. I have to believe that in all that seething mass of people there on the West Coast, and other places, at least five hundred retired couples can easily be found who will like what we have to offer. They will have accumulated assets and retirement incomes to fuel our town's needs. I am betting my own money and reputation on that belief."

"It sounds reasonable," Lenore Grayson agreed. "It has attracted Harold and me here. We are almost certain to retire in Kansas or in some like place. The term, 'amenities' will be a consideration in determining where that place will be. Tell us about those amenities."

John looked out the window at the almost perfect fall day and smiled. "Shall we begin with the climate?" he asked.

"We know about the climate," Harold Grayson said with a small chuckle. "If it could be like this every day, Oklahoma would be overrun with people trying to find a place here."

"If it were like this every day," John countered, "we would have no bad weather to compare it to. As it is, we can be very sure that we will have a genuine appreciation for this kind of weather. Most people tend to be tolerant of the negatives if they know there will be an equal number of positives. And, too, a steady succession of lovely days tends to get boring. For myself, I find some ugly weather to be a nice break from the usual humdrum."

"I can agree with that," Harold said. "I remember how a good thunder storm used to fill me with awe. And a prairie blizzard was like a holiday to break up the boring routines of everyday life. We just hunkered down by our warm fires and waited for the storm to blow itself out."

Lenore and Meg looked at each other and smiled. "What about the tornadoes?" Meg asked. "Do we just hunker down and wait for them to pass?"

"Yes," Harold replied, "just like we have done on several occasions with California earthquakes. Either way, we have to consider our chances. I think I prefer to take my chances with the tornadoes. Most of the time we can get out of their way or take shelter, but the quakes don't give us any warning or places of safety. Most people will agree to that. So let's get to the other amenities.

What else, John, can we expect to get by living in this new town?"

John was quick to reply. "Space, clean smog-free air, freedom from traffic, relaxed easy country living, and a community center in which to enjoy civic and social camaraderie. And we plan to have the usual conveniences of a grocery store, medical clinic, pharmacy, service stations, churches, and school. Some of those items may be added when a city government is established to assess the needs and wishes of its citizens. I can imagine myself as being happy as an old horse knee-deep in clover, and I will do all I can to make it happen."

"At what price, John? If it proves to be out of the reach of us ordinary mortals, it won't happen."

"I'm planning on the average eighty by one hundred twenty-five foot lot to cost about four to five thousand dollars, with a thousand of that to be reserved for construction of the city center. The cost of homes will vary according to the wishes of the various residents. I estimate that the average cost per unit to be about twenty to twenty-five thousand total. The cost of the lots must come back to Meg and me for land and development costs. We need to recover our investment and a fair per cent for the planning and the work we are doing."

The Graysons appeared surprised. Their value base was that of booming California, where similar lots and building costs were much higher. They looked at each other and then at John. "Are you sure, John?" Harold asked. "That seems very low. Why don't you consider the higher figure just in case your costs are higher than expected? Then, if things go better, you can always add something else to the amenities later on."

"I've told John that," Meg said, "but he is so afraid he might be accused of being profit motivated and that some people will lose their faith in his real motives."

"The people whom he hopes to reach in California won't," Harold Grayson said. "On the contrary, they are more apt to be wary of what they may consider a rip-off scheme because of the low costs. Be reasonable, John. I think that anything less than five thousand dollars per lot is too cheap."

"Okay, I'll rethink my prices," John said. "But before that happens, let's go out and check the merchandise."

The rest of that morning, they walked over the area where the surveyors had staked out the platted town-site. John pointed out the street locations and their systematic convergence into a larger area that was to be the city center. The Graysons asked many questions, and John and Meg were quick to explain their vision of a modern town to be built according to plan rather than haphazard needs. The Graysons were favorably impressed and asked that two joining lots close to the city center be reserved for them. It was their vote of confidence that John's dream was a valid one.

"We will be closing our agency in California this winter," Harold said. "If possible, we would like to begin building a home here next spring or summer. In the meantime, we will continue to represent you out there if you want us to do so."

"In what capacity? John asked.

Harold turned to his wife. "What do you think, Lenore? How much do we want to get involved in this?"

She studied the pattern of stakes that marked their future home-site. The grassy turf became a green lawn surrounding a ranch style brick house overlooking the wide expanse of valley through which meandered the sliver of water and sand that Meg had once dubbed Arena Del Rio. Other houses were there, too, with their fences, hedges, and shrubs marking their territories and giving them identities. And she saw people their also—nameless faceless people, busy with their chosen tasks and hobbies as they shouted friendly greetings to others of their kind—contented people leisurely pursuing the quiet tenor of their retirement.

"If this is to be our home for the rest of our lives," she said at last, "we must dedicate ourselves to it completely as John and Meg are doing. We must believe in it! Anything less is tantamount to failure. And we cannot afford to fail, Harold. I think that we should make it our contribution to see that people like ourselves will want to share in this dream. If John and Meg will keep us informed about their progress here, we can promote and handle sales of lots to prospective buyers on the West Coast."

"On commission?" Meg asked.

"Only enough to cover our costs, I would think," Harold Grayson proposed. "Say five percent for advertising and escrow fees. Anyone interested enough to make a trip here to see what they are buying will have to do as we are doing and pay their travel costs. If they choose to deal directly with John and Meg, no commission will be involved."

"That sounds very fair," John said. He looked to Meg for her approval.

She nodded. "Very fair. That kind of help is exactly what we need!" she exclaimed. "We will keep you supplied with photographs and details as we move forward."

"Do you want a contract?" Harold asked.

John squinted his question to Meg. "Only if you do," she said. "We will make this a project of faith and trust. You send us the buyers, and we will sign the papers."

"With hand shakes all around?"

"Agreed!" John said.

"That's pretty trusting, John!"

"Not really, I've checked you out! What about yourself?"

"No problem. We have your business history, past and present."

"It will be a pleasure to do business with you and Lenore."

"And to be neighbors?"

"And to be neighbors," John said.

Chapter 7

Throughout the winter of 1970-71, work on the new town went steadily forward. Only occasional spells of bad weather shut the operation down, and by spring, the leveling and grading, the earth moving and filling of gullies, the installation of utility lines were all done. An ample supply of sweet underground water, fed by the Canadian River seeping through its sand, had been confirmed. Then, the initial paving of streets began just in time to accommodate the arrival of the curious locals and the serious home seekers drawn in by Grayson Realtors' publicity efforts in California.

That spring was especially beautiful. It was almost as if Oklahoma knew that guests from far places were arriving and that she should be especially nice. John and Meg greeted them all warmly and gave the sporadic procession of out of state visitors food and lodging in the upstairs rooms of the old house. A second hand juke box was installed on the front porch, and the lyrics from the well remembered musical, *OKLAHOMA,* were played intermittently throughout each day. Blue birds nesting in a small cavity above the porch and mockingbirds singing their endless variations of birdsong from the big cedar trees gave the lovely May days an almost magical quality. The inclement days of winter and the severe heat of August were small considerations to those who were caught up in such a magical time. By the end of June, one hundred forty-seven lots had been sold and new houses were being constructed. The Graysons were the first to occupy one of those homes. Chisholm, Oklahoma was being born.

But it was with some difficulty, for the summer heat dried up the surge of visitors from California. Even so, enough local traffic of older people from the towns and villages still came, unmindful of the heat and the incessant strident chirrings of the cicadas. By the fall of that year, forty-one more lots were sold, and John and Meg put the Graysons in charge of the project.

They were tired. They instructed their contractor to begin construction of the new house John had promised to build. Harold Grayson promised to keep check on the contractor. Meg handed over the plans that she had been working on in her spare moments, and they went traveling in a new motor home. They spent most of the winter in Arizona and found life there too tedious. Needing to take care of business interests in California, they relaxed there until another spring found them back in their new house on the fringes of Chisholm. They were home again, rested and relaxed, with the firm knowledge that they would have little need to spend so much time away from there dream community. Chisholm had become their haven. Though they still sorrowed for the past and their lost grandson, they began to think more and more of their present and future.

It was Meg's choice to return to The Hosanna Baptist Church in El Reno where she and John had gone in an attempt to become a part of their grandson's life. Though their motives had been a bit devious, they had enjoyed the quiet devotional atmosphere. They had left feeling soothed and rested by the experience, even though the painful rejection of their attempts to see their grandson had discouraged them from returning. The pain of that rejection was still with them. It would never quite go away. But Angela had married her handsome young minister and gone with him to serve in a church in the Oklahoma border town of Abrams. Meg had seen the announcement of their marriage in the El Reno newspaper. When a second announcement of his new assignment as pastor to the Abrams church appeared a week later, both John and she knew that their grandson was definitely lost to them.

"I want to go back," she said. "Why don't we go, John?"

"Angela's mother and grandmother are still there," he reminded her. "Can you be comfortable there?"

"Of course! I am not going to be intimidated by their attitudes. If they want to be sociable, fine! Who knows? Maybe they will loosen up and tell us something about Caroll."

"Carl!" John said.

"Whatever," she snipped. "We aren't likely to know what his mother calls him. But maybe we can learn something about how he is getting along."

"I think about him every day, Meg. I guess I want him to replace Frank who I still miss so much. I know that sounds foolish, but I have an empty feeling that keeps me sorrowful and lonely."

"It's not foolish, John. I miss Frank, too. And I am hoping that when things have had a chance to level out, Angela will understand and relent. Maybe her husband will understand and shame her into being more reasonable. According to the paper's account of their marriage, he is a local boy with his roots in El Reno. It is not likely that he will completely separate himself from his family and friends. We may see them again sometime."

"Maybe," John agreed. "We will go back to the church next Sunday."

Sunday morning dawned clear and sparkling after a day of rain on Saturday. Meg looked out from the big bedroom window and murmured, "Oh, what a beautiful day! Rogers and Hammerstein were right." She stepped out to an adjoining room which she had been using as a temporary office and switched on a record player. Almost immediately, the music and lyrics of their songs were being piped throughout the house.

John pushed back the bed covers and grinned. A sense of well being and pride surged through him. He was realizing his dream. Oklahoma was enfolding him as a mother might enfold a son who had been away too long. With a glad cry of exultation, he rose quickly and went to join his wife. For a long moment, they stood together at the window and gloried in the sights and sounds of the morning. Mist lay over the line of trees that marked the valley below them, and dew sparkled from the newly landscaped yard and lawn where noisy kingbirds were already busy with their nesting in a locust tree. Crows cawed from somewhere in the line of cedars, and from a distance beyond came the faint gobble of a tom turkey.

"Oh, John," Meg whimpered tearfully. "It is just as you said.

This is so much more beautiful than Las Vegas or Los Angeles. I will never complain about the weather here again as long as I know that we will have times like this!"

"Soak it up, Meg," John said gleefully. "When the winds of March and the heat of August come, we can remember this and appreciate the promise of a perfect day. It's much too beautiful to waste inside. Let's get ready and have breakfast in town before we go to church."

"I'll be ready in an hour," she whispered.

And, as they had two years earlier, they joined the late stragglers and were ushered into the quiet interior of the church to sit as guests for the morning warship and sermon. Recognizing them as strangers, the usher asked, "Would you like to sign our guest book?"

"Certainly," Meg replied, and she stepped to the small table inside the door. John stood quietly by and watched her write *Mr. & Mrs. John Claiborne, Chisholm, Okla.*

The usher's face broke into a wide smile. "How wonderful," she exclaimed. "We have been hearing so much about you and your town. It is such a pleasure to have you here. Where would you like to sit?"

Meg let her eyes sweep over the expanse of pews. The big church was almost filled. It seemed as if the loveliness of the day had sparked some human urge to express gratitude. The sunshine saints and stormy day sinners were out in force. John shrugged. "Can you find us a place near the center? I can hear better there."

"Come with me," the usher murmured. "We will squeeze you in somewhere." She led them toward the center where she found a pew holding not only people but also several large handbags. As curious observers studied the late arrivals, she bent toward them. "This is Mr. and Mrs Claiborne from Chisholm," she said brightly. "I hope we can make room for them."

One of the ladies with the handbags sniffed. Somewhat reluctantly, they both lifted the handbags to their laps and edged themselves over to fill the created space. "It will crowd us up a bit," one grumbled.

Only then did Meg recognize the two as Angela's mother and grandmother. She felt her gut tighten for a moment and was about to apologize and request a different location. But a tinge of anger strengthened her resolve. "This will be just fine," she said. She eased herself down and John squeezed in beside her.

"If the present company gets boring, we can sleep," he whispered in her ear. "And we can be the first to get out when it's over." Straight faced, Meg very lightly nudged him with her elbow.

Not once during most of the long service, did either of the pairs acknowledge the other. Though Meg could feel the body warmth emanating from the person on her left, it was as if an invisible wall was also there to keep them separate and apart. No Christian warmth could get through it, for none was there. Even the lovely music from the organ and church choir could not dissipate the chill that persisted on into the sermon. Its topic was an appropriate one.

"Love thy neighbor as thyself, even as God loves all of us," the minister admonished. Meg could bear it no longer. She half turned to her left and murmured, "Good morning, Mrs. Watts. I hope that we can be neighbors." She got no response. Only the aging mother smiled and nodded to acknowledge the gesture of goodwill.

When the service was over, Meg repeated her greeting and good wishes to the old mother who had lagged behind her daughter. Tight lipped and angry, Mrs. Corbett apologized for her daughter's attitude. She lingered for some moments on the walk just outside the door and tearfully begged for forgiveness. "Bertha has had many disappointments in her life," she explained, "but I cannot excuse her behavior. We have had many talks, but she has not listened to me. Now with Angela gone, she makes my life miserable. She lives in my house, but never considers me as one whose wishes are important."

"We understand, Mrs. Corbett," Meg soothed. "We do not want to intrude, but we want very much to hear about little Carroll. He is our grandson, too, and he is the only one we have. Can we meet with you sometime for some news about him? Or can we give you a call occasionally?"

"I would like that," the old lady said. "If Bertha takes the call, ask for me. If she hangs up, keep calling. And don't hesitate to come to the house. It is mine, and you will be welcome any time. If Bertha chooses to be hateful, it will be her sin, not mine!"

Meg gave her a warm hug. "We might do that, Mrs. Corbett," she assured her. "You have been very kind, and we appreciate it. And may God bless you for your understanding. We will stay in touch."

They escorted her to the car where Bertha waited glumly. John opened the door for her, nodded to the younger woman, and helped the old lady in. When they were gone, he turned to Meg and shook his head sorrowfully. "That's an unhappy old lady," he muttered. "She does not deserve her nasty daughter."

"I know," Meg agreed. "And she isn't very strong. It's so sad to see her old and failing while enduring her daughter and granddaughter's hateful ways. I think that we should visit her some day."

"Would that only increase her problem?" John asked. "I suspect that Bertha might be more hateful if she saw us as getting too friendly with her mother."

"That Bertha is a strange one," Meg said, "and I suspect that you may be right. I'll call her on the phone soon and see what develops."

But that was not to be. Subsequent calls were not answered. Several weeks later, an operator informed them that the number was no longer in service. Very much concerned, they drove to the family residence to investigate. The house was vacant and a new "For Sale" sign was posted in the front yard. A dowdy neighbor from across the street saw John peering into the vacant house and wandered over. "Kin I hep you all?" he drawled.

"Why, yes, I hope you can," John said. "We are looking for Mrs. Corbitt who was living here."

"She ain't no more," the neighbor declared. "The old lady died sudden like three weeks ago. Fell over dead with a stroke."

Meg gasped. "How can that be?" she exclaimed. "We saw her at church about a month ago!"

"Hit don't take long to die with one of them strokes," the neighbor said with a shrug. "She 'uz fine one minute and dead the next. I reckon her strange daughter hepped to bring it on. I heard 'em arguin' in the yard one evening, and next thing I knew the ambulance crew came screechin' in. They hauled the old lady away, but she 'uz already gone."

"And her daughter? What happened to her?" Meg asked.

"Don't really know, I don't," the man said. "The granddaughter— that 'us the pretty one who married the Califonia feller that got hisself killed by the hoodlums—well, she came home with her preacher husband and they buried the old woman. That 'uz after the funeral, of course, which 'uz in their church. They 'uz here near ten days, I reckon, 'fore they loaded up the house goods and left again."

"I didn't see anything about it in the paper," Meg said, "and I usually read all the local news."

"People like them don't get much notice," the neighbor said.

"Did you know them very well?"

"As well they would let me. I been here nigh five years, and they never said more than a few words to me. The old lady was kinda nice, but the other two—" He shook his head sadly.

"We're sorry to hear it," John broke in. "We appreciate your help." He turned to Meg and muttered, "Let's go, Meg. There's nothing we can do here."

They returned to their car and as they drove away, Meg quavered, "I feel that we have buried Frank all over again."

"Except that it's more like our grandson being buried now," John said.

Chapter 8

In the spring of 1973, most of the remaining lots were sold. And the newly organized town council, with John Claiborne acting as mayor, met to plan the long awaited city center. Citizen meetings gave all residents opportunities to be heard. Special requests that would cause costs to exceed the funds already available were hashed over and accepted or rejected. In the end, a city hall and adjuncts of fire station and magistrate's hall were included as a part of a larger complex. A large general-purpose hall and auditorium with a spacious parking area completed the project. The cost was considerable, but funds reserved from the sale of the lots were adequate to pay for it all with a nice profit for the Claibornes. They had been generous with their time but not foolish with their money. Throughout the project, they had been determined to make some profit from their efforts and to make their town an independent entity.

John and Meg Claiborne, with their good friends, the Graysons, had seen the culmination of their dream. Their town of some eight hundred retired people and almost a hundred young families was a reality. Problems were few, and people were, as John had hoped, living out their retirement years with a degree of contentment seldom found in congested cities. These were the nearest to being family that the aging couple could hope for. Only the lack of a living heir or near relative to give their lives a deeper sense of continuity was lacking, and they sorrowed often for the grandson who had been denied the right to share their dream in such a natural setting. Resigned to their loss, they dedicated themselves to finish the making of their town. A few more details needed their attention. Then they could rest.

But the news had spread throughout the state that a new idea for retirement living was being implemented in Canadian County.

Hopeful retirees still came to investigate.

John and Meg were both gratified and puzzled by their success. Their dream had created a larger need than they had anticipated. Obviously, the law of supply and demand had caught up with them. Inspired by the need, they decided to expand their boundaries by developing an addition along the town's northwestern border. By the end of that year, two hundred more lots were made available. By 1980, the ten year old town was mature with a tax base. The steady flow of retirement money in the hands of an industrious generation now seeking relaxed living had fed its needs. Taxes on their properties would take care of future needs.

"We must stop it here," John said to Meg when the last of the houses were being built. "I wanted a town, not a city."

"When does a town become a city, John?" Meg asked.

John looked out the window at the orderly arrangement of houses extending beyond the long ridge bordering the river valley. He sighed. "When it becomes segmented into neighborhoods so separate from each other that they are no longer town oriented. We can become that way if we keep growing. Then we will need industry to fuel an economy that has exceeded its ability to survive on retirement money alone. Taxes will become excessive. Discontent will follow, and we will be like a thousand other small towns struggling to survive. We need to stop any further growth."

"And how can we do that if people keep coming to share our good fortune. They know that we have a special place here. With all the available space around us, how can we deny them a little bit of that space?"

Her husband was quietly meditative, his voice wistful. "When we came here in April of 1970, the population on this ridge was two—just you and me, Meg. Now, only ten years later, it's almost eighteen hundred. We are crowding out the other creatures that also need space. Just because we are human, and can, is no reason for us to take away their space. What we have done for these eighteen hundred people, I now want to do for the wildlife. I want to surround Chisholm with a wildlife refuge."

She smiled. "I sort of thought you would do that, John. I've seen how protective you are of the deer and turkeys when they wandered into town."

"They don't do that much anymore," he said ruefully. "People complain about them browsing their shrubs and messing up their lawns. They use their dogs to drive them away. Now we've got a pack of half wild dogs roaming clear to the river."

"And people are becoming impatient with the coyotes and armadillos, the crows and the raccoons, John. What about those? Armadillos are horrible creatures to deal with when they dig and tear up lawns and flower beds. They have ideas of their own about whose space they are invading."

"And that's to be expected, Meg. People and wildlife don't mix very well. That's the reason I want to donate most of the surrounding area to the game department for a refuge. I'll build a chain fence around three sides of the town if the department will administer and supervise the refuge."

"The fence won't keep the armadillos out," Meg protested.

"That's for sure! They are like people. They move in and take over. And people will have to handle the problem just like they handle any varmints that become too pushy."

"I'm glad you said that. I killed one with a shovel yesterday when I found it digging under my rose bush. Then I felt guilty and worried all day about what you might think. It's the first time in my life that I ever killed anything bigger than a fly or spider!"

John grinned. "My wife is adapting to the ways of the wild," he chuckled. "Keep your shovel handy. When you kill one armadillo, two more will drop in to see what the commotion is all about."

"I'll hire some neighbor kid to trap and release them down by the river."

"Like who? Kids these days are too wrapped up in their own lives to bother with our problems."

"The Graysons' grandson came in yesterday to spend the summer. He will help me."

"Bobby Grayson? I didn't know he was coming back again. Last summer, he was a typical city boy scared of his own shadow. I had a devil of a time teaching him to bait his line when I took him down to the lake fishing. At the sight of an ugly old armadillo, he'll run crying home to his Grandma Grayson."

Meg looked at her husband with some exasperation. "Why John, I'm ashamed of you. The boy had never been fishing before. Besides, he was only thirteen at the time."

"Just thirteen? He is such a skinny little kid! I thought he was about nine or ten."

"Wrong, John! He's only a year younger than Carrol."

"You mean Carl! Ah, now, Meg, Carl is a lot older than the Grayson boy! Carl will be sixteen next December."

Meg's eyes grew wistful. She sighed and sniffed. "Sixteen!" she whispered, "and half way through high school. Soon he'll be grown, and we don't even know what he looks like. I wonder if he ever comes back to El Reno?"

"I read the local news every day," John reminded her. "So do you. I study the weekly church calendar every Saturday for some item that might refer to Angela and her husband. And I have seen nothing. I'm beginning to believe that they have never been back or that they have purposely suppressed the knowledge of being back."

"I don't think that, John," Meg objected. "Why would they do that? We certainly haven't done anything to cause them to do it."

"It's only a short day's drive from Abrams to El Reno," John mused. "Maybe we should drive down there someday and see what we can learn."

Meg looked at him owlishly and hooted. "Oh, no, John! That would be an invasion of privacy. I am perfectly willing to wait a few more years. Then, when Carrol is an adult and his own man, we can think about a reunion of sorts. For now, I think you need to use your grandfatherly skills to take Bobby Grayson and some of the other small boys under your wing."

"I might be too busy," her husband alibied. "And that could get out of hand. I can imagine how an endless procession of kids might be showing up every day wanting to go fishing."

"You are making excuses, John," Meg chided. "All you have to do is set aside one particular day and let the kids know that it will be their day to go fishing, or rambling, or swimming, or whatever. If the weather is bad, take them to the game room at the center to play pool. I think you need that, and I think they need you. The ponds and lakes we made will be off limits to them when the refuge is finalized. They will need a sponsor. You could be a big influence on the kids whose parents are off working and unable to take them fishing."

John looked out the big upstairs window. He could see the small ponds and the bigger lake shining in the morning sun. Fish were there in the depths, and the waters on hot days were clean and cool. He had not taken the time to enjoy his outdoors as he would have liked. There had always seemed to be some reason not to.

And he thought of his childhood when there had been little but the Canadian River's scanty waters to provide opportunities for fishing and swimming. Wildlife had become almost extinct, and hunting was not an option. Also, the daily farm work had been too demanding, and he had seldom taken the time in those days to pursue those outdoor activities. Now, he had them all at his backdoor. And he thought about the young ones in his new town with time to waste and few chances to enjoy those activities that had been denied to him when he was their age. He looked at Meg and nodded.

"Beginning next week, Friday will be fun day for Chisholm's kids," he said. "I will enlist the help of other old guys like me, and we will organize outings for the kids."

Meg looked at him over her glasses. "Just boys?" she ask.

"Well, now, Meg, girls can't very well go skinny dipping with the boys!"

"Then, what about the girls? They need activities, too!"

"Yes? Keep talking, Meg! They also need to be supervised."

She shook her head in dismay. "I didn't consider that very carefully," she sniffed.

"You need them , Meg. They need you. What day will be best for you?"

She looked at him and smiled. "Friday will be perfect," she said.

Chapter 9

Those were good years for the town of Chisholm. Almost without exception, its senior population had found retirement there to be immensely rewarding. It had all the amenities that John and Meg had spoken about that fall day in 1970 when their good friends, the Graysons, had come to consider their vision of a new town. The town had space, clean air, and relaxed living. But its people had more than that! They had friends and neighbors with similar backgrounds and values, and Meg said that she wished they had named the town Amity or Congeniality, or some such descriptive title to better describe its character.

"I like Chisholm," John said. "It doesn't promise anything. If things start going wrong, no one will be cynical about a place and name that seem to be mismatched."

"You are being cynical at this moment," Meg observed. "What could possibly go wrong now?"

"Hardship always follows the good times," John mused. "Bad weather, depression, war. The Vietnam disaster is finally over, but the cold war and the nuclear threat is still with us! We can't live in our complacent little town forever without experiencing some of the sorrows that plague the world. I guess I am getting old and pessimistic, Meg."

"I know," she agreed, "I worry about those, too, but worry doesn't make them go away. I worried about Frank when the Las Vegas trouble came up. It didn't help. And I worried about the loss of our grandson to two neurotic women who took him away. That didn't help either. Now he is living somewhere completely unaware that we exist. So what is the purpose of worrying?"

"No purpose whatever," he admitted. "Occasionally, I need to be reminded of that, Meg. I guess that I really am getting old."

"Sixty-nine is not old for one who is as healthy as you are, John. Age is a state of mind!"

"Maybe it's the big seven zero facing me next month!" John admitted. "And Carl will be twenty-one in December. We have a grandson who is now a man, Meg. Maybe we should think about trying to find him."

"Maybe, we should," Meg murmured.

But some whimsy of fate saved them from that difficult problem. Later that month, when Meg read the weekly section of church news, the announcement of Pastor Herman Keller's retirement leaped out at her. The aging minister of the Hosanna Baptist Church was retiring and was to be replaced by Reverend Robert Haynes, a former member and assistant pastor of the church. "Reverend Haynes will assume his pastoral duties on July 1," the announcement said. "He will be accompanied by his wife, Angela, daughters, Naomi and Ruth, and their son Carl, a recent graduate of Dallas Baptist Seminary. Son Carl will serve in the temporary capacity of assistant to his father until he receives a pastorate assignment of his own. Hosanna Baptist Church is fortunate to have such dedicated servants of God serving its membership. Though we will be reluctant to lose Reverend Keller as our pastor, we eagerly welcome the return of Reverend Haynes and his family."

John received the news with mixed feelings. His grandson was now a man. "How can I ever think of a grown man as being my grandson?" he asked ruefully.

Meg sniffed. "I don't know, John," she murmured. "It will seem strange seeing a little boy in a man's body. And that is how I remember him, a little boy on a red tricycle. Most likely he will not remember us at all."

"Or maybe he won't care," John shrugged. "His mother has probably tried her best to remove us from his memories. But that won't keep us from making an effort to reconnect if we want to take the chance of rejection."

"I would be very nervous about doing that openly," Meg mused.

"But if we started to go to church there now before they arrived, we could establish our presence as being legitimate. But that seems a bit sneaky. Besides, I feel at home in our Sunday services at the Chisholm Community Hall. I think I would prefer to drop in again as a visitors when we know that they are back in town."

John agreed, and when the last Sunday in June came, they appeared at the Hosanna Baptist Church entrance and were greeted by the new minister himself. The intervening years had erased any remembrance of the two people he had once greeted there almost fifteen years before. Their names murmured softly struck no chord of recognition, and they signed the guest register and were ushered to seats along the outer aisle. They sat quietly watching the throng of people gradually filling the empty pews.

It was an eager and expectant congregation assembled to express its regrets for the loss of one pastor and the pleasure of gaining another. Meg and John, like dozens of others who had not been in the church in years, settled back and waited. Their reasons for coming, though, were different. They had come to see a grandson long lost to them.

"Will Angela recognize us?" John whispered in Meg's ear.

"She will if she can pick us out of the crowd of faces," Meg whispered back. "We haven't changed that much, have we?"

"Fifteen years," John murmured. He studied the many faces around them and saw no one who appeared familiar to him. And when the robed choir was ushered in to fill their places on the large platform altar, Angela was no where in evidence. Only when the service had begun and the retiring pastor was making introductions, did she stand with her husband and family of three children. A handsome young man stood among them.

Meg gasped and looked at her husband. "It's Carl," she whispered.

"Oh, God," John whimpered, "he looks so much like Frank!"

"Oh yes, so much like Frank!" she breathed.

They said little more during the entire service. Nor did they hear much of the sermon, as their attention was so completely centered on the happy family sitting in the special section reserved for those of favored status. The usual hymns were sung, prayers offered, the retiring pastor's last sermon delivered. All were background effects. Their emotions were of a different sort—a kind of reverence reserved for an only son lost and an only grandson returned. When the final "Amen" was uttered and the ushers systematically dismissed the congregation, they solemnly moved with the others to make their exit through the wide front doors. And their grandson was there, unknowing and unaware of whose hands he shook that day. "We are so glad you have come," he said and his voice was almost as familiar to Meg as the voice of her dead son.

"You are Caroll?" she asked.

He looked at her curiously and smiled, "Carl," he corrected. "Carl Haynes. I will be acting as the assistant pastor for a while."

"Yes, we have heard. It is so nice to see you after all these years."

"Thank you. I hope that you will come again."

"We will do that, Pastor Claiborne," Meg murmured as she moved away.

The young man looked startled as John, stern faced and silent, shook the proffered hand and joined his wife. As they walked down the wide walk, he turned to her and asked, "What did you say to him, Meg?"

"He invited us to come again, and I said, 'We will do that Pastor Claiborne!' "

"It must have rung a bell. I think you may have gotten his attention. But why?"

"He called himself 'Carl Haynes'! I wanted him to know who he really is!"

"He was Carl Claiborne for only six years," John chided. "He has been Carl Haynes for fifteen. Maybe he won't remember who he was fifteen years ago."

"He will remember. I added our telephone number when I signed the guest register. I am hoping that he may get curious and check through the list of signatures," Meg assured him. "He is our grandson, and he is very smart. In time, he will wonder, for I will always call him that whenever we come here. He will remember, and he will know who we are."

"I hope so!" John said.

It was mid-afternoon that Sunday when their telephone rang. It was muted, but loud enough to rouse John from his afternoon nap in the big easy chair. Meg, reading the Sunday paper, looked at John. "I wonder who that could be?" she mused. She lifted the receiver from its cradle and murmured, "Hello."

The reply was hesitant and a bit nervous. "Hello," a voice said. "Is this the Claiborne residence?"

Meg's response was equally hesitant and nervous. *It's too much to expect that he would call so soon,* she thought. She caught her breath and swallowed. "Yes," she replied into the mouthpiece.

"John and Meg Claiborne?"

Meg looked across the room at John. "What is it, Meg," he asked.

Wide eyed, she mouthed a silent answer, "I'm not sure." Then, she took a deep breath and said to the caller, "Yes, this is Meg Claiborne."

"Mrs. Claiborne, this Carl Haynes, who spoke with you briefly at the church this morning," the caller said. "I was confused by the remarks you made and checked the guest list hoping to learn who you might be. My father, who died when I was very young, was Frank Claiborne. Could you by chance be a relative of his?"

Meg's reply was tear laden. "I am his mother," she quavered.

"Dear God in Heaven," the voice said reverently. "You must be my grandmother!"

Meg was almost distraught as she fought for control. "Yes," she whimpered. "John and I are your grandparents. We have missed you so much these many years. Please come to see us if you can. It's not far, and we have so much to talk about!"

"Yes, we have so much to talk about! I will come this afternoon if you wish. I can be there in an hour."

"We would like that very much," was Meg's tearful reply. "You will find us in the red brick house at the east end of the row of big cedar trees."

The voice was almost exultant. "You can be sure that I will be there," it said.

John grunted. "My God, Meg!" he stammered. "Was that really him?"

Meg looked at her husband and nodded. She straightened her glasses and laid aside the newspaper that she still held folded in her lap. "Yes," she sobbed. "That was Carl. And he will be here in an hour."

He swallowed hard and took a deep breath. His words were raspy and elongated. "That was really Carl?" he muttered.

Wide-eyed and unbelieving, Meg rose to join her husband. Seeing his shocked disbelief, she went to sit on the arm of his chair. He cuddled her like a parent would a child and stroked her hair. For some moments, she wept as her body quivered and shook. "We must remain calm," he soothed. "We cannot let any hostilities toward his mother and the other grandmother influence us."

"He will have questions," Meg sniffed. "How can we answer honestly without making his mother look bad in his eyes?"

"Honestly and discreetly," he insisted. "He must be made to understand her insecurity and desperation during that ill-fated marriage. And he must be made to realize that we have been innocent victims of her misunderstanding."

"That will be difficult," Meg sighed, "but we must let his mother bear the burden of that misunderstanding. He will have to sort out the facts of her explanations."

"He can do that, I think," John said. "Now, let's get ourselves calmed down for his arrival."

It was an impatient sixty minutes for them to prepare for a role so long denied them. They were up and down, pacing and peering out the window. Meg made countless visits to her bedroom mirror to improve her grandmotherly image, while John performed trivial tasks to correct imagined cosmetic flaws about the big front yard. Both were as nervous as giddy parents awaiting the birth of their first child.

Finally, after repeated glances through the big front window, John saw the small compact automobile turn slowly into the curved driveway. It eased itself onto the concrete garage ramp and stopped.

"It's Carl!" Meg whispered. Her face puckered, and she trembled as she reached for the doorknob. Through unashamed tears, she quavered, "Come in, Carl."

Uncertain and confused, the young man looked down at her, and fifteen years were instantly erased. "Grandmother?" he asked.

Almost distraught, she nodded and opened her arms to embrace him. "Our grandson has returned to us," she whimpered.

John, close behind her, put his arms around them both and exclaimed, "Fifteen years! Our grandson is now a man. It has been such a long time, Carl!"

"Yes, a lost time, Grandfather. We must not let that happen again. Now, I need to know how it happened."

"We will need to talk about that," John said, his voice wispy and fluttery. "But it's too hot out here. We need to go inside where it is cool." He led them in and solemnly motioned toward a seat on the big couch. "Sit there, Carl." He glanced at Meg and took a deep breath. "Maybe your grandmother will get us something cool to drink."

"Only ice water for me," Carl said. His voice was tight, with a hint of hoarseness to indicate his nervousness. He looked at John and chewed his lower lip to curtail a need to weep. Tears were clouding his eyes, and John recognized, then, his own buried sorrow and his own need. He eased himself down beside the grandson, who now was a man, and embraced him. When Meg returned, she found them there mutually emptying themselves of their sorrow. She joined them, and long wordless minutes passed as the healing began.

"It is good to weep," she soothed. "It washes away our sorrows. It tenderizes our souls."

John brushed away his tears and murmured, "Yes. I am puzzled why we do it so seldom. This is the first time I have wept since Frank died. But, then I have had only a few deep sorrows, and those have been mitigated by a wise and wonderful wife."

Carl sniffed, smiled, and quoted scripture "'Weeping may endure for a night, but joy cometh in the morning!' In my childish way, I wept when my father was killed. I wept and wondered why such a thing could happen. My mother has told me about it, but I still do not understand. For these many years, I have wept silently for his loss and for the grandparents who I thought had abandoned me. Now, I weep openly, but I still do not understand. Perhaps with that understanding, I can still know the joy that 'cometh in the morning.'"

"We did not abandon you, Carl," his grandmother affirmed. "We have been here in this place since 1970 waiting."

"I did not know that," Carl protested. He shook his head sadly as though to shake away the memory of rejection. His face contorted as he pled for answers. "And I need to know. Please help me understand."

John looked at Meg. She understood his dilemma. The answers their grandson so desperately needed could cement his relation with his grandparents. But, at the same time, they could create a feeling of betrayal by the mother he loved and cherished. *I must try to do one without doing the other,* she thought.

"You must first know that your mother greatly misunderstood who and what your father was when she met and married him," she said through her tears. "You need to understand that!"

"Yes, Grandmother, I will understand. Please go on,"

"Her world was much different from his," she sniffed. "She did not understand his, and he did not understand hers." She shook her head sadly at the memory and stopped to wipe her eyes.

"I am so sorry, Grandmother," Carl apologized. "I don't mean to bring up old sorrows."

"Of course you don't," she quavered, "but it is something that you must know. They married too hastily. Their marriage was of the flesh and not of the spirit. Her world was the world of El Reno and, more specifically, her church. His was the world of the West Coast, the world of business. Neither could adjust to the other's world."

"Was my father a bad person, Grandmother? Was he sinful? Mother claims that he never knew Christ and salvation, and that he is almost certainly in Hell. Was he really that sinful?" The words came in a tremulous mixture of fear and desperation so shocking to John that he could barely withhold his anger.

Meg saw and understood. She could not risk an explosive retort so early in this reunion with a grandson whom they had been missing so long. Her reply was spontaneous and sorrowful. "Only in your mother's eyes," she said. "He was our son. We knew who he was. He was kind and considerate. He was honest. He was a good man who loved life, and he loved you above everything else."

"And my mother? Did he love her?"

"When they were first married, he adored her," Meg assured him. "But she was desperately unhappy in Las Vegas. He was very busy in the construction business and incapable of being the husband she required. She needed an eight to five worker who came home each evening to devote all of his other time to her. She wanted him home on weekends and in church with her on Sundays. That was her world as she had learned it in El Reno. It has been her world since his death and her return to Oklahoma. And I am sure that she has been very happy with it since."

Carl nodded his head in agreement. "Mother has had a wonderful life with my stepfather. They have been so compatible that I have never known them to quarrel. Sometimes they may argue about doctrine, and mother usually wins. But they do not quarrel. He has been a good father to me."

"I am sure he has," Meg agreed. "And you must not forget that, Carl. If your real father had lived, your parents would have divorced eventually. The fault was not theirs individually, except in the very beginning when they chose to marry. They listened to their hearts instead of their heads. As for his being in Hell, your mother should be reminded that she should not judge lest she be judged!"

Carl nodded and gave Meg a long searching look. His face puckered. "I still do not know why I have not been a part of your life. My mother has never told me why."

Meg breathed a deep sigh. She returned her grandson's searching look and lay her hand gently against his cheek. "If I tell you why," she murmured, "you must promise that you will not place the blame on anyone except the unfortunate decisions of your parents to marry. What has happened since that time has been a result of that decision. It left your mother disappointed and bitter, and she could not free herself from the fear that your grandparents, John and I, might bring the Las Vegas world back here to influence her child. She greatly feared our presence and did not want us to be a part of your life. We would only be constant reminders of the husband whom she felt we had failed to rear properly. She did not want the sinful ways of our world to become a part of her world. She requested that we stay out of your life."

"Oh, my poor mother," Carl whispered. "I wonder why God could let that happen to her."

"Perhaps it was because God wanted you to be born," Meg suggested. "You wouldn't have been, you know, if they hadn't married." She risked a quick look at her husband. His face screwed into a frown. She gave him a quick sly wink, picked up the empty water glasses, and disappeared into the kitchen.

Carl did not return for Sunday evening service in his church that night. John and Meg urged him to spend the night with them, and he agreed. He called his mother, and explained why he would be absent. She was not happy, and suggested that he should be with his family to share in the fellowship being tendered by his church to welcome them back.

"I have another family here which I have not seen since I was five years old," he explained. "It will be very inconsiderate if I do not spend more time with them. I will be home tomorrow morning."

He heard the long sigh and waited for his mother's response. When it came, it was soft and subdued. "Very well," she said. "We will expect you home tomorrow."

Chapter 10

Carl left his grandparents' house the next morning much relieved. The reasons for their absence from his life had been explained. They were not bad people as his mother had sometimes hinted. Their love for him had been well demonstrated, and their religious devotion, though not remarkable, was evident. And more than anything, Meg's explanation for his mother's fears and consequent actions had been reasonable though unfounded. He would bear her no ill will for actions resulting from those fears.

Perhaps I can bring about a reconciliation, he thought.

But his mother's dismay and sharp disapproval would make any relationship with her former in-laws most unlikely. Her reasons were simply stated. "They are not my kind of people," she sniffed. "I could never be comfortable in their presence."

"How do you know, Mother? You have not seen them in fifteen years. For such a wonderful Christian lady, you seem to have a most un-Christian attitude," her son chided.

Angela's mood seemed to soften. She chewed her lower lip and looked as if she might cry. "Must my son talk to his mother like that?" she whimpered.

He stifled his remorse with a soft, reassuring reminder. "Your son is also a pastor. He cannot turn away from behavior that he sincerely believes to be wrong. Your prejudices effectively bear false witness against good people, Mother! They were so glad to see me that they wept unashamedly, and we had plenty of remorse and sorrow to share. I must and will become a part of their lives!"

Her reply was superficially contrite. "I am sorry, Carl. I will try to do better. I must remember that you are a man now as well as a pastor. I should no longer need to protect you from outside influences. I can only trust that God will lead you in the ways of righteousness.

If you feel that you must keep seeing your grandparents, be guarded in matters of Gospel. I will trust you to do that."

He was silent a long time, and the old questions of his mother's prejudicial attitude were like worms squirming in his mind. *Why?* he ask himself. *Why is she so biased against these two people when in most things she is Christian in her beliefs?*

He recalled his grandmother's admonition about judging. He rose, stepped before her, and searched her face. His words were gentle but accusing. "Judge not lest you be judged," he said. "If your judgment of my grandparents proves to be valid, I will know in time. If they prove to be shallow and petty, I will lose a bit of my love and respect for you. I shall spend a lot of time in their house if they welcome me there. You need not fear their influence on my faith. It is strong, and only God Himself can alter it."

She shrugged and turned away. "Be that as it may," she muttered.

And so the new relationship with his grandparents began. To their mutual satisfaction, it was to be a happy one, separate and apart from the one he shared with his El Reno parents. And the two lives that he was required to live were also vastly different. Where one was under the watchful eyes of his religious parents, the other was more relaxed and interspersed with the wonders of an outdoors he had previously not experienced. He and John, and sometimes Meg, were frequent visitors to the ponds and small lakes dotting the new wildlife refuge bordering the town. Sometimes they fished, sometimes they swam, and sometimes they were like young children rambling the river breaks to examine its wildlife mysteries. But in all those excursions, the grandson never failed to comment on the wonders of those mysteries and God's part in creating them. Religion was seldom ever very far from his mind.

One day, when Meg had declined to go with them, they were lolling in the cool shade of a cottonwood tree by the river. Following a long silence in their many discussions about life, Carl fixed a long solemn gaze on his grandfather's face and asked the ultimate question so uppermost in an evangelist's mind. It was meant to be casual, but John recognized the concern and sincerity that had generated it. "Have you been saved, Grandfather?" his grandson asked.

For some moments, John remained unresponsive as he continued to study the slow circling movements of a hawk high above in the summer sky. He didn't like the question and wished that he could ignore it. He considered it invasive and pondered how best to divert it. He casually slapped at a mosquito buzzing near his face, sighed, and sat up. "I didn't know I was lost," he commented.

Carl smiled. He was aware of the attempt to dismiss the question, and briefly considered dropping the matter. But the aging grandfather at his side was in danger of losing his soul if death should come unexpectedly as it had fifteen years earlier to his son, Frank. *I cannot let that happen,* he thought. *It is my responsibility to save him.* He flipped an ant from his trousers leg and said solemnly, "We are all lost," he chided. "Scripture says that we are born in sin and that Christ was sent to save us. But it also says that we can be born again and be freed from sin and have eternal life. I really think you should consider that, and make your peace with God. Life is uncertain, you know."

"Well, now," Grandfather said thoughtfully as he scratched the stubble on his chin, "I never knew that we had a falling out. We've gotten along just fine so far, and I don't see any problem."

Carl brushed another ant from his clothing and asked softly, "Don't you believe in God's miracle of salvation, Grandfather?"

The older man looked at his grandson quizzically. His words were gentle but stern. "My beliefs are numbered among several billion others existing in this world," he said. "That makes them pretty personal. I will promise to respect yours if you will promise to respect mine. Now, it's beginning to get hot. Let's go home."

Somewhat subdued, Carl sighed and agreed. "I promise," he said.

When the days grew too hot and dry, they retreated to the cool entertainment center in the heart of the town to join others for games of dominoes, cards, or pool. Even the strict Baptist code did not rule out those as being unwholesome and sinful when enjoyed with fellowship and camaraderie. The citizens of Chisholm had been careful to encourage wholesome behavior and quick to discourage disorderly conduct. Almost every day was fellowship day in Chisholm.

But on Sunday mornings, those earthly pleasures were set aside, and the entire hall was given over to a quiet informal kind of worship. Nondenominational and undemanding, that time had been pleasing to both John and Meg. The singing was spirited, the organ music relaxing, and the prayers as private and devout as each participant deemed adequate. Lay speakers were often asked to lead discussion groups to air matters of faith and conduct. Sin, as a special topic, seldom merited a place on the morning agenda.

For Carl, the Sunday service was a new experience. It lacked the more fervent Baptist determination to keep Satan and his temptations at bay. And he questioned the lack of a choir to give elegance to the old hymns, and a minister to breathe life into God's messages. *Perhaps,* he thought, *this is to be my ministry.*

In the fall of that year, while a few months short of his twenty-first birthday, he bared those thoughts to his grandmother. He had sensed that she might be more receptive to his idea than his grandfather, and he was right. She took the bit in her teeth and expressed her pleasure.

"What a wonderful idea!" she exclaimed. "Have you mentioned this to your grandfather?"

"Not yet," he said, "I wanted to get your reaction first. He may think that I'm too young to pastor a church."

"What do you think, Carl? That may be more important than what I or John think."

He looked out the big front window at his grandfather puttering in the yard. "I feel the calling," he murmured. "My entire life has been leading to the ministry. Chisholm and I need each other. I hope Grandfather will understand and give his support."

Meg watched her husband rolling up a hose for winter storage. She stepped to the screen door and called, "John, will you come in for a moment? We have something to discuss." She saw him lay the hose aside and brush off his clothing.

He squinted through the screen and mildly complained at having his morning chores interrupted. "Can it wait?" he asked. "I want to put this yard stuff away."

"Now, you just forget that for now," Meg scolded. "When you hear what Caroll has in mind, you will see why."

"*Carl,* Grandmother!" John mimicked. He looked at Carl and grinned.

"Okay, Grandfather! *Carl* it is," Meg replied sternly. "Now, you listen up! Tell him, Carl."

Encouraged by Meg's bravado, Carl took a quick breath and exhaled. "We need a church in Chisholm, Grandfather," he said calmly.

"We have a church," was John's quick reply. "It meets every Sunday at 9:30 AM. You should know. You've been there, remember?"

"I mean a real church, Grandfather," Carl hastily explained. "A real church house with a choir and a real live minister."

"And wherever are we to find all that?" John asked as he peered over his glasses.

"From we, the people," Carl said. "We organize the choir, we build the church, and we engage a minister. The minister comes ready-made. I will be the minister. I regret the short notice."

John chuckled. "I know," he said. "I expected to hear you say that someday. Only, I didn't expect to hear it quite so soon. But all of that takes a lot of planning and a lot of work. Aren't you a bit young for that kind of responsibility?"

Meg interceded. "Now, you better not be difficult about this, John. The people here need a church, and they need a minister. They keep talking about it, but nothing ever happens. Our hall is full nearly every Sunday. Most of those people will support a new church."

"She is right, Grandfather," Carl said hopefully.

"Most of the time she is," John agreed, "and I believe she is now. But before I go along with the idea, I have to lay out a few conditions. The first one is to quit calling me *Grandfather*! The title makes me feel like an aging member of Parliament."

Carl's cautious demeanor changed to one of mirth. "It is a title of respect," he said solemnly. "What title does Lord Claiborne prefer?"

"Any thing is better than *Grandfather!*" John grumbled. "Take your pick—Gramps, Grandad, Grampa. And pick out one for your Gramma!"

"Leave me out of the name game, please," Meg objected. "I happen to like *Grandmother.* It has an element of sophistication that suits me. Now, let's get on with the other conditions. We will need to present the idea to our church congregation. Its support is crucial. Then we can move on to the planning stage. We will do that Sunday morning."

"Who do you mean by 'WE'?" John asked. "That will make a difference to some people who won't want to change to a denominational kind of church organization. They will be much more receptive to ideas that come from inside the group. Even then, they will have a lot of choices to muddle through."

"I am Baptist by background and training," Carl stressed. "If I am to head the church, I would expect it to be that denomination."

"That is what I mean," John explained. "If you are expecting to get a congregation from the Chisholm population, you will have to win them over to your side first. You can't do that in a single meeting next Sunday morning."

Meg was thoughtful. She gave her husband a long thoughtful look. "So, what would you suggest?" she asked.

"I think that Carl should become an active member of the present church," John replied. "He should volunteer to act as pastor until he gets an assignment elsewhere. I have heard him lead the group several times and have been impressed. He needs to establish himself first and make himself indispensable to the group. Then, and only then, will ideas for a new church be seriously considered."

"And what if I should get an assignment in the meantime?" Carl asked. "Would my plans for a church here have to be put on hold for later? I need employment now. My funds are limited. I need an income."

John nodded to indicate his understanding. "The State Wildlife

Federation needs an on site supervisor of our local Game Reserve," he said. "It doesn't pay a great deal, but you could live here at no cost, and the salary should be ample to let you survive. And I have plenty of work around this house and grounds to keep you busy much of the time if you want to do it."

"I would like that," Carl said. "I worked my way through high school and college mowing lawns and doing landscaping. I want to be as useful and self-supporting as possible until the trust fund from my father's insurance matures five years from now. I will turn twenty-six then, and the interest alone will be almost enough to make me independent."

Again John nodded. "Until then, we can be conditioning the Chisholm people for your church idea. Then, it all has to be planned and financed. That could easily take several years. But it must be made to appear that it is the people's idea first and foremost," he warned.

"Isn't that a bit of subterfuge, Grampa?" Carl suggested. "I don't want to be a part of anything tricky. And I don't want to wait five or six years. The need is now, and I think that the time is ripe for a new church."

John chuckled. He looked at his grandson, and his admiration for his honesty was evident. "Nor do I," he said. "But this will be more like diplomacy than subterfuge. You will need support, and the surest way of getting support is to develop trust and confidence first. That cannot be dishonest. It will be far more dishonest to disregard the other people's concerns. They must not be led to believe that a young ambitious upstart has come into their town to push change to suit his agenda. It must be their agenda first and yours second. I expect that they might not want to wait too long either. Don't you agree?"

"Yes, I do," Carl agreed. "I wouldn't want to create doubt or suspicion about my motives. I like the people here, and I want them to like me. What you say makes sense. But I am anxious to get things started. They can sow the seed, and together we can all nourish the growing plant."

Meg nodded approvingly. "That is a nice parable," she exclaimed, "and spoken like a real minister. I am so anxious for next Sunday to come."

"Ah, yes," Carl said, "I am, too!"

Chapter 11

When Sunday morning came, Carl's determination to build a proper church in Chisholm was strengthened further. The nearly full hall gave him an idea. *If I can help fill it to overflowing,* he thought, *the people themselves will demand a new church. They will be the driving force, and I will be the driver.* When he was asked to give the closing prayer, his message about fellowship and community spirit contained a faint hint that the civic hall could not always be expected to accommodate the people's needs. The first seeds were planted.

He became active in planning and organizing youth groups, and by that fall, he was delivering short, low key Sunday sermons. He made himself personable, and was extra careful to remain sincere but undemanding in his expectations about people's beliefs. He deliberately avoided any hint of fundamentalist church dogma. His listeners were impressed.

By Christmas time, he was seeing faces that he had not seen previously. People filled the hall for the Nativity scene, leaving others standing in doorways to hear the young pastor's sermon about joy, faith, and hope. He concluded his message with these words, "This joyous Christmas season I have but one sadness. Like the infant Jesus lying in the stable manger because there was no room at the inn, many good people are standing just outside our doors because we have insufficient room to make them welcome at this beautiful service. Some may have turned away with disappointment, their little children puzzled by our own lack of room for them at this holiest of occasions. We must not let this happen ever again. My sadness, my faith, and my hope I am dedicating to the planning and construction of a facility that will make this the last time for this to occur in the town of Chisholm. I am asking this congregation to join with me in this enterprise!"

Quick action followed that eventful Christmas season, and in January a church committee was formed to make serious plans for a new church. Meg, John, the Graysons, and two others agreed to begin a feasibility study of costs, building sites, and building plans. Meg was chosen to lead the study, and with her past experience in project planning, the plans materialized amazingly fast. The Graysons took charge of fundraising and financing, while Carl and John considered a number of locations to accommodate the church grounds. By June, they were ready to break ground on a twenty-acre tract overlooking the river valley.

"Here at the west end of the cedar grove is a most appropriate spot," John had said earlier. "A church needs space and the beauty of landscaping to surround it. Parking alone requires several acres. And the church grounds need to include a parsonage, playgrounds, and picnic areas. Most town churches don't have all that, and they should." He was silent for a long moment as he considered the vacated wheat field where he had as a youth helped his father and brother with the harvests. Then he pointed to the field beyond the fence's far boundary. "Perhaps," he added, "more space can be made available there if this twenty acre block in not enough."

Carl was astonished. "How could we possibly ever need so much?" he had asked. "Ten acres is ample. Even the largest of churches don't have as much. And we have to consider cost and maintenance, Grandpa!"

"I understand," the older man said, "but I am paranoid about space. I guess I lived too long on the West Coast where there was never enough of it. I came back here where we have plenty and can afford to be generous with it. I try to remind myself that time has a way of changing our expectations, and we find too late that we have let ourselves to be boxed into tiny cubicles. Who knows what unforeseen circumstances may arise in the next century?"

"I can't imagine anything so huge that it may require more space than a few acres, Grandpa," Carl chided. "The Baptist Church in El Reno doesn't cover half a city block, and it does just fine. People park on the street or in lots nearer to downtown and walk."

"Maybe when the church was built, those old guys didn't think beyond next week," John suggested. "Then the town grew and boxed the church in leaving no room for it to expand. Maybe we should think about the church growing faster than the town. Then it may need the extra space."

"A church with a few hundred people won't need twenty acres, Grandpa. Certainly not forty acres!" Carl protested.

"Probably not," John agreed. "But the land won't move, and it can still do what it's been doing, growing wheat. It's your Grandma's and mine, and I expect that it will one day be yours. I don't need to think about that now. What we do need to do is to think about the church's access to roads and utilities. That means that it should be located here where Chisholm Road comes in from Hinton Junction. That will give easy access from both Interstate and most of the streets into Chisholm. It will be visible from several directions and can add a lot of class to our landscape if we can ever get an agreement on its architecture."

"Should it be closer into town, Grandpa?" Carl asked. "This seems to be a bit far from the center of things."

"No other space is left closer in, Carl," Grandpa explained. "And it's only five or ten minutes out. This higher ground is a perfect spot if you can imagine the things like landscaping that will come later. The main building can go here, and fifty yards or so farther over is just the right spot for the parsonage. And the spire of the church can be seen from miles in all directions. We'll bring Grandma out and get her opinion. She has an eye for that sort of thing. She will steer us right!"

"You make it seem so exciting, Gramps! When do you think we can get started?"

"As soon as the architect finishes the plans and the county gives the final approval. You have raised enough money to get started. Meg says that she has enough pledges from reliable people to finish if we are careful. I have donated the land, and I don't want to finance the project further. I don't want it to be my church. It must be the Chisholm people's church."

"And mine, too, Grandpa! When the time comes, I want to put in several thousand from my trust fund. I would like that to be a sort of memorial to the father I never got to know."

The older man grew wistful. He turned to his grandson and lay his hand on his shoulder. "You are so much like him," he murmured. "He had a kind of enthusiasm for life that I see in you. And I have missed him so much. So has his mother. Now, we are so thankful to have you in our lives after so many lost years. I hope that your mother understands that."

Carl was thoughtful. He sighed and chewed his lower lip. "Mama doesn't say much," he said softly. "She continues to be a mystery to me. It's almost as if she doesn't know how to admit her mistakes of the past. But I am praying for guidance and patience. I would like so much for her to know you and Grandma as I have come to know you."

"We would like that, too," John said. "We would like for both her and your stepfather to be present at the opening dedication. It will mean so much to us all."

Chapter 12

When they broke ground for the new church in early August, nearly a hundred people were on hand for a prayer service. Many of the retired citizens with building skills lingered to volunteer their time and expertise to the project. All were enrolled and placed on call for future times when they could be most useful. John acted as contractor for the special construction phases, and Meg and Carl began to organize groups for final decoration of the interior. But one important part of that final phase remained unresolved. What was to be the outcome of the stained glass windows that nearly all of the new parishioners so passionately wanted?

The issue had not been one of those hotly debated in the many long hours of the planning phase. In fact, it had been an assumed priority by even the few who had been loudly critical of other design decisions. "We want the kind of church that our community can be proud of," they had said. "A brand new church with ordinary windows will be like a brand new minister who comes to Sunday service in a laborer's clothing!" The issue, then, had never been contested. But when the bid from the artisans in Indiana had come in mid-September, a new reality sobered the visionaries. The building committee was out of money, and they had few other resources to tap. The few remaining pledges had been for landscaping of the grounds and the paving of the parking areas. Even Carl's planned ten thousand dollar contribution from his Trust Fund would not be available for four more years. The project was in danger of stalling because a favored priority had no funds to implement it. All eyes were turned on the elderly, affluent grandparents.

"We could solve the problem quite easily," Meg proposed. "The stained glass windows could be a memorial contribution from us."

"With our names displayed prominently for all the other

parishioners to see? I wouldn't like that," Carl protested.

"Then leave the name display off," Meg suggested.

"I have wanted to believe that this is a people project," John stressed. "Now, it seems that we are expected to be parents of the thing. I believe that the people need to study their real priorities. Do they want a house of worship, or do they want a material show place to impress those who happen to come for church services. Stained glass windows are just another example of human vanity, which in itself is supposed to be a sin. Why can't they just put in plain glass windows that we can see through?"

"Wow!" Meg chortled. "Do I hear Ebenezer Scrooge talking? Or is it the Grinch who stole Christmas? Get real, John! People go to church for all kinds of reasons! And one of those is to sit in a quiet peaceful setting away from all of the cares of the outside world. You and I do that. You know we do. How often do you really hear the pastor's words about sin and salvation?"

"Well, I can be content just looking out over the countryside," her husband countered. "Through those big clear glass windows, I'll be able to see the whole Canadian Valley. I happen to believe that God spends most of his time out there. How can people expect to see Him through stained glass windows? They do more to shut Him out than to shut Him in."

Meg frowned. Her arched brows and squinted eyes indicated that her barometric pressure was rising. "You can't be serious, John?" she chided.

John read her barometer and backed off. His little boy smirk was the kind he liked to use when he knew he was being unreasonable. "Not really," he chuckled. "But if we bail them out on the stained glass windows, I think it should be a business deal. We should loan the money at a low interest rate for five years. That way it will not be our church. It will be theirs, and they will feel an obligation to make payments to keep it theirs."

Meg sighed her relief. "You had me worried for a bit," she admitted. "I will agree to that on condition that if our deaths should occur before the loan is paid, the remaining balance is to be marked paid in full."

John gave her a warm hug and muttered, "Your agreement is hereby accepted. The church will have its stained glass windows. Now, I think we should talk about the need for storm cellars. No one has mentioned it yet, but it is bound to come up sooner or later—probably later after the project is finished or about the time tornado season comes next spring. But the time to consider things like that is now. Don't you think, Meg?"

"I did mention that in one of our planning sessions, John. Several favored tabling the question until later. Carl's response was to the effect that he preferred to rely on his faith that God would take care of the righteous. Our discussion ended there, and hasn't come up again."

John could not keep the scorn from his voice. "Great Crap!" he snorted. "In the matter of faith, that boy has too much! I'm pretty sure that a tornado rampaging up tornado alley won't be asking God for directions. I suspect that I had better take care of that myself."

Meg smiled and eyed her husband with a knowing look. "I thought you would," she chided. "I think there should be a special area in the basement for people in the church during tornado alerts. And a shelter like the one we have outside our back door, should be located just outside the back door of the parsonage."

"I'll put it in the construction plans," agreed John. "Then I'll sit back and wait until tornado season to see whether discretion or faith wins out"

"Your sarcasm overwhelms me, John. But don't let it overwhelm Carl. Though his faith may be a little extreme, it sustains him and energizes his dream. Let's keep it that way."

"I suppose," he muttered. "Maybe it will be contagious and infect the rest of us."

"I think it already has," Meg murmured.

Though it was in the hottest part of the summer, work progressed amazingly well. While final work was being completed inside, crews began the grading and landscaping of the grounds. Except for some painting and cleaning, the modern structure with its red brick veneer, stained glass windows, and white spire and bell tower was complete enough for a special Thanksgiving service. A final opening and dedication service was to follow at Christmas time. Carl's plea of the previous year was being realized. He had a church and a substantial following from the town and surrounding rural areas. But in one respect, it was not as he had hoped. He was Southern Baptist, and his pastorate at the behest of his flock was to be nondenominational.

That was also a big disappointment to his mother and stepfather. To them, the Baptist faith was paramount, and they struggled with the concept that their Baptist son should be the pastor of a nondenominational church. But Carl had explained that it was necessary to gain community support and funding, and they had reluctantly accepted his explanation.

He had seen the reluctance of the Chisholm citizenry to support a dominating religious organization that had remained very conservative in its attitudes toward a more modern society. Many women, still smarting from their years spent in the male dominated work force, were not at all sympathetic toward a male dominated church hierarchy. They wanted a church, but they wanted it on their terms. And Carl quickly learned that his dream of a church with the elaborate name of Hosanna Baptist Church of Chisholm was not possible without the united effort of the local citizenry. The church, despite some lingering objections, became known instead as the Chisholm Evangelical Church.

Carl considered it to be a nice compromise and believed that he could conscientiously serve as its pastor. His Baptist parents had accepted that. They were present at the formal dedication in December. It was their first attempt to renew a relationship with Angela's former husband's parents. Fortunately, the great press of people and their excitement at seeing the culmination of a community effort, mingled with the glow of the Christmas season, kept the reunion from being strained and clumsy. Greetings were murmured, regrets were hinted at, and attentions were diverted toward the happiness of the occasion. Nothing more would ever be said about a former time of suspicion and separation.

The first year of Carl's pastorate was immensely rewarding. He carefully tailored his sermons to the wishes of his congregation and was careful not to push his Baptist conservatism onto the church agenda. At the same time, he tried to fulfill the promise of the church name and strove diligently to win souls for his Christ. In that he succeeded, for he was sincere without being pushy, and he was adept in his counseling and persistent in helping with people's problems. The number of young people in his congregation increased, and soon a noticeable number of young parents were also helping to fill the four rows of pews.

His popularity with the younger set was helped further by his decision to marry the young woman whom he had known since his early childhood. Young, very pretty, and devout in her religious views, she was an ideal choice to fill the role of the young pastor's wife. Only one small detail existed to raise a few prudish eyebrows.

She was a daughter of his stepfather's brother. Consequently, she had the same surname as Carl's adoptive name. In many eyes, that made the two of them cousins, though no blood relationship was involved. Theirs had been a long clan relationship in which brothers, sisters, aunts, uncles, even grandparents had frequently mingled together to celebrate holidays and anniversaries and, on occasions of illness and death, to commiserate their sorrows. She was family in one respect and not family in another. But others on both sides understood the difference and were happy to see the romance develop and come to flower. His mother particularly approved, for she remembered her own rash choice of a husband almost twenty-five years earlier. Her son would be saved from such a mistake.

And, yet, she was a bit uncomfortable with the unusual joining of two in holy matrimony with the same surnames and family affiliations. To her, it seemed contrary to Baptist traditions, somehow. *Isn't a wife supposed to surrender her name and take that of her husband?* she ask herself. *But how can Vernalee Haynes do that when her betrothed is also named Haynes?*

The more she thought about that, the more she found herself being opposed to the plan of her son's marriage to Vernalee Haynes, and Carl was quick to sense her changing attitude. His solution was to do what he had been secretly considering since that Sunday morning when his grandmother had slyly addressed him as Pastor Claiborne. Shortly after his twenty-second birthday, he filed a request in the county court to have his birth name replace his adoptive name. When all of the legal work was done, he became Carl Claiborne again. That damaged a few egos, but it solved the problem very nicely. In June of 1986, Vernalee Haynes became Vernalee Claiborne in a conservative ceremony in the Baptist Church in El Reno. John and Meg Claiborne had not only regained their grandson but also his real name. And the petty doubts of the critics were no longer valid contentions. No one came forward that morning to protest the union of two young lovers who were so well suited for each other.

Vernalee Haynes was a beautiful young woman. Quiet and unassuming, she reflected the conservative Baptist faith that had shaped her. Her one purpose in life was to be the faithful and loving wife to a godly man and to bear his children. As such she was a perfect choice for the young minister whose calling was also so much her own. He loved his young wife dearly, and together, they settled into the new parsonage to fulfill their commitments to their god and themselves.

Chapter 13

An adage in the whimsy of modern skeptics states quite simply, "If anything can go wrong, it probably will." Though often quoted facetiously, it still contains a greater truth than its proponents realize. In this chaotic world where perfection is more of an ideal than a fact, human bliss is never permanent. Something will go wrong eventually. In the long chain of earthly events, the human saga must go through its periods of both bliss and tragedy, though exactly when, or to whom, or to what extent each is to occur, will be as haphazard as the winds that blow. Chaos will ever make it so, and bad things will happen even to the best of people. It was to be so for Carl Claiborne and his beloved wife, Vernalee.

For six years, they led blissful lives as close to Heaven as anyone could wish. Well aware of their many blessings, they often commented on the goodness of their God and his benevolent love for them. Almost always, they ended such discussions with prayers of thanksgiving, after which the happy couple resumed their euphoric lives, renewed and much refreshed.

A year after their marriage, their first child was born. Saved from the disappointment and pain of a tragically flawed birth, Carl held her perfect form in his arms for the first time and naively murmured, "How could anyone seeing such a miracle ever doubt the existence of God?" They named her Carolee and gloried in the reality of her being of their own flesh and blood. "God is so good!" was their careful reminder to each other.

The miracle of their first child was followed two years later by the birth of a second daughter, as perfect and lovable in every way as their first born. To honor the infant's two generation grandmothers, Meg and Angela, the giddy young parents christened her Megan, and whatever old wounds remained from that earlier hurtful time were healed and forgotten. Angela and her El Reno family became frequent visitors in the Claiborne homes. Carl, remembering those earlier times, whispered, "Praise God for this miracle of forgiveness!"

He had become the esteemed and much admired leader of a new church recently sprung from the prairie soil. He had also made himself prominent in the civic affairs of Chisholm and the social welfare work of Canadian County. And the Claiborne family name was being heard often in political circles and in discussion groups throughout central Oklahoma. It would be on many tongues two years later throughout the same area, but for entirely different reasons.

In 1992, following a long, blustery winter that had lingered on into March, spring made its triumphant entry into the Canadian River valley. It arrived quite modestly but soon demonstrated its usual grandeur. Overhead, migrating waterfowl honked their way back to their Arctic nesting grounds, while, far below them, the electrifying color of redbud trees burst along the wooded hillsides. Soon, then, a tinge of tender green appeared along the long line of the willow and cottonwood groves along the river. Spring's promise was being kept.

And in the hearts and minds of people, still weary from the drab colorless winter, new hope and new energy welled up in response to that promise. Spring was a time for renewal—a time for reminding impatient humans that things needed to be done, a critical time that could not be wasted. The wintertime of waiting was over!

It was also the time when Baptist leaders often planned their conferences for organizing summer programs and activities. Such a conference to deal specifically with youth problems was to be held in the Baptist Convention Hall in Nashville, Tennessee. Scheduled at a slack time between Easter and Memorial Day, it was an opportunity for Carl and his stepfather to take a break from their busy lives. They made plans to attend. They would take a plane on Monday morning and spend three days in Nashville before returning home the following Friday.

With her two maturing daughters deeply involved with their end-of-the-year school work, Angela decided to spend those days with her daughter-in-law and grandchildren in the church parsonage in

Chisholm. She looked forward to being there to help with the small children and to be a buffer against Vernalee's loneliness during her husband's absence.

"How wonderful!" Carl exclaimed, just before departing for the Oklahoma City airport. "Grandmother and Gramps Claiborne invited them to come over to their house for the week, but that would mean packing the kids and their clothes into their space, and I am not sure those old people need their lives disrupted like that. It will be so nice for her to be here with Vernalee and the kids." He looked at his stepfather and added, "Don't you think, Dad?"

"I do, indeed," agreed the older man. "Things could get a little dull in El Reno with me gone. Here, your mother can spend some quality time with them. I do think, though, that a few words of prayer for their safe keeping are in order before we go."

"Oh, of course," Carl exclaimed. "I wouldn't think of leaving without a prayer." He motioned to the group around him. His anxious wife, his two wide-eyed wondering children, and his solemn-faced mother closed ranks and formed a circle. His words were quiet and almost plaintive.

"Gracious and Loving God," he murmured. "We leave these whom we love most dearly in thy keeping. Bless them and protect them in our absence. Lead them in the ways of thy teachings and keep them safe from all evils. These things we do solemnly pray, O Lord, Amen!"

And the closing "Amen" was passed around the circle and repeated by even tiny two year old, Megan. Then, they all embraced, and the two ministers, one older and seasoned, one younger and tender, loaded their luggage and departed. They could not see or anticipate the two huge air masses poised many miles away waiting to test their awful energies, one against the other, in the hours ahead.

But the meteorologists in their weather stations could. Their sophisticated equipment and data from other stations indicated very troublesome conditions in the two envelopes of air covering the northwestern sector. One weather expert studied the latest charts and maps and said solemnly, "If those two air masses come together like I think they will, we will have a squall line stretching all the way to eastern Kansas. We had better be getting some weather alerts into the pipeline!"

But the flawless spring day kept many of the retired Chisholm residents out of doors doing yard work or making home repairs. John and Meg Claiborne spent the day edging their lawn and pruning trees and shrubbery. Vernalee and Angela took the children on a picnic outing and ate their lunches on the church playgrounds. Not being addicted to worldly affairs and the scandals of television, they never turned on the television set that entire day and evening. Completely unaware of the two jousting air masses marshaling their forces over the Texas Panhandle, they tucked the two little girls into their beds at ten o'clock. Soon, they too were sleeping soundly in their own beds, oblivious of the ugly squall line approaching like an invading avenger to wreck its havoc across the western outskirts of John and Meg Claiborne's peaceful little town. The tornado that it spawned, though not huge, had skipped its way through the Oklahoma farmlands, lifting itself across the low swales and shallow valleys and, just as dawn was breaking, setting itself down again on the ridges as it approached the Canadian Valley.

Angela heard the rumble of its thunder, listened for a moment, and went back to sleep. The sound of thunder was of little concern to her. Forty-seven years in her native Oklahoma had conditioned her to thunderstorms. And killer tornadoes were not likely to threaten righteous people.

But Vernalee responded differently. A much louder clap of thunder warned her awake. Groggy with sleep, she hurried to her west bedroom window and peered out. She heard the distant wail of sirens from the direction of the town and a loud hissing sound that quickly grew to an ominous crescendo of noise similar to that of an approaching freight train. She saw the big cedars twisting and writhing as though being attacked by monstrous forces, and she heard debris from their broken branches hammering the house. In a panic, she screamed a warning into Angela's room and rushed to rouse her sleeping children. In seconds she had them out of their beds, half-carrying, half dragging them, as she fled toward the side door. Angela met her there and took possession of tiny Megan. "The shelter!" she shrieked. "We must get into the shelter!" But it was too late. As she was reaching for the door latch, the west wall exploded into the vacuum of the tornado's throat, and they were all sucked into the mass of swirling debris. The last words Vernalee would ever hear were her mother-in-law's agonized plea, "Dear God in Heaven!" Angela collapsed across the unopened shelter door and shuddered.

And the uncomprehending funnel cloud moved on to destroy three more houses on the northwest fringe of the sleeping town. But their inhabitants, forewarned by the awful noise, had escaped into the safety of their underground shelters. Its energy dissipated by the lower elevation, the tornado lifted its ugly funnel and disappeared into the void of the valley below. Its work was done.

Chapter 14

The same clap of thunder that had awakened Vernalee also awakened Meg and John, two blocks farther east. But even at that greater distance, the sound was ominous and unmistakable. "Oh, my God, Meg! I think it's a tornado!" He saw the red glow of his bedside clock with the numbers giving the time as 5:05. He rose hastily and rushed to the window. Meg gasped and grabbed her robe. Together, they peered into the uncertain light of a dawn corrupted by chaotic violence. They, too, noted the awful agony of the huge cedars being whipped to a frenzy by unseen forces. Brilliant lightning illuminated the distant church standing staunchly at the very edge of the storm's fury. Beyond it, out of their view, sat the smaller parsonage, its fate and its inhabitants' fate indiscernible.

"Get in the shelter!" John shouted, as the house lights flickered. "The tornado may be headed this way! For God's sake, hurry, Meg!"

"But what about the others, John?" she wailed. "They will need help!"

"Later, Meg! We can do nothing until the funnel passes!" He grabbed her arm and hurried her to the downstairs doorway. With the wind gusting and whipping at their clothing and remnants of storm debris drifting around them, they lifted the shelter lid and escaped into the dark silent interior. Together, they huddled in the safety of that artificial void trying to comprehend the awful violence they had just witnessed. Meg moaned and trembled uncontrollably in her husband's arms, and over and over again she moaned, "The parsonage, John? What about the parsonage?"

"Maybe they got into the shelter, Meg," he gasped. "We can't know until the storm has passed. I'll check as soon as it's possible for me to get over there." He remembered the switch for the shelter lights and fumbled his way in the inky darkness to where he thought it would be. His hand brushed the wall and found it. He felt its downward movement under the pressure of his fingers. But no light came on.

"I was afraid of that," he croaked. "The power lines must be down." He reached below and located the shelf where he knew the emergency lantern and matches were stored. They were there, and he breathed a relieved sigh. "Now, I really know what it must be like to be blind," he mumbled. In the yellow glow of a kitchen match, he lifted the lantern globe and lit the wick. In the smoky light, he saw Meg, disheveled and distraught, huddled against the shelter wall. He hung the lantern from a hook in the ceiling and went to her. Not since the death of their son, Frank, twenty-three years earlier, had he seen her so stricken. He led her to the small settee and helped her to sit down. She clung to him and wept silently. Gently, he stroked her hair until her trembling stopped.

"I must go to the parsonage," he said.

"Yes," she moaned, "we must both go. Perhaps they had time to get into the shelter."

"Let me check to see what the damned tornado is doing," he said heavily. He stepped up the steep narrow stairs and lifted the lid. It was almost quiet outside with only the drumming sound of rain to suggest the storm's passing. A subdued wind continued to harass the bedraggled line of cedars, and a belated dawn was giving enough light to make visible the distant church. Its appearance was more like that of a bedraggled hound that had been left unsheltered in the storm. The tall white steeple was broken and hanging like a flag at half-mast from the front roof peak. The stained glass windows had been sucked out, leaving empty eyes to stare vacantly into the shroud of rain. A siren's wail added an eerie emphasis to the littered scene.

He squinted at his wristwatch. It was 5: 20. "Fifteen minutes," he muttered. "A lousy fifteen minutes!" Solemnly, he returned to look down at his wife of fifty years and shook his head. "It doesn't look good, Meg. It sure doesn't look good. I think the rescue people are on their way, and it's best that we be there too."

"Yes, we need to be there," she whimpered. "But we need to

dress first. I can be ready in a few minutes. Silently, she followed him through the rain into their undamaged house. When they were hastily dressed and in John's pickup truck, they heard the moaning siren marking its difficult passage on the street paralleling the line of bedraggled cedars. In fear-stricken silence, they followed the emergency vehicle as it threaded its way past downed trees and broken limbs. When they came to the church parking area, both vehicles stopped there to assess the best and quickest way to reach the parsonage still half a block away.

Through the falling rain and the breaking dawn, they could see the awful wreckage that had once been a beautiful annex to the still standing church. No evidence of life was there. Meg dropped her head and wept. John consoled her with the thought that the two women and the small girls might still be in the shelter. "I have got to go find them," he gritted. "The rescue guys may need some direction. You wait here until I get back." He checked his watch again. "5:28," he groaned.

He paused to exchange information with the four-man rescue unit. He knew them all and their conversation was quick and animated. "Have part of your crew follow me," he pleaded. "If anyone is alive over there, they need us now. The rest can bring the ambulance when they find a way to get through."

He broke into a jog trot toward the demolished parsonage. Two paramedics with their stretcher and medical kits trailed close behind him. Oblivious of the falling rain, they followed the wide littered walkway toward the ruined parsonage. Avoiding the clutter that the tornado had left behind, they soon came to the hulking wreckage. John went directly to where he knew the storm cellar to be, and his last hope for his grandson's beloved family vanished more quickly than had the rampaging tornado. The wet sodden form of Angela, still in her nightclothes, lay across the shelter's entry lid. The young medic quickly knelt beside her and checked for vital signs.

He shook his head sadly. "We are too late, John," he murmured. Then he corrected himself. "No," he said, pointing to a segment of broken tree branch piercing her chest. "She never had a chance. We

couldn't have helped her. My guess is that she died almost instantly."
He rose and chewed at his lower lip. "What about the others? How
many were here with her?"

John choked on the words. "Her daughter-in-law and two small
girls." He turned away and wept.

"I'm sorry, John," the medic whispered. Then he turned his
attention to the piles of wreckage sucked out by the storm. His hasty
search revealed the body of a young woman and a small child lying
partly covered in a scattering of bricks and segment of wall lying a
short distance away. He had barely finished his quick examination
when the rest of his unit and the ambulance arrived. In stunned silence,
John heard him say, "Three victims accounted for. All dead! One
still unaccounted for."

He could bear no more. *Meg must not see this,* he thought. In a
half stupor, he plodded back toward his parked truck. Seeing his
approach, she went to meet him. His woeful demeanor was enough
to stiffen her for the terrible news. "Oh, dear God," she wailed.

"They are all lost," he whispered, his words barely audible.

"All?" she wept. "Even the little ones?"

"Little Megan, hasn't been found yet, but I think she is dead with
the rest. I didn't want you to see."

Meg's only reply was an anguished cry. "Why? Dear God, why?"
It became a litany unanswered and unanswerable, as, like two
zombies, they returned to the sanctuary of their own house. There,
they sat, stunned and unmoving, alternately muttering and weeping
until they heard a subdued tapping on their door. John took a deep
breath, rose, and went to answer the caller's summons to what he
assumed would be more bad news. The medic stood there, bare
headed and long faced. "Mavis Hobbs and her husband, Floyd, from
the church were the first to get the bad news and wanted to come
along," he said. "We are sorry to bother you at such a difficult time,
John. But we need some help on who we should be calling about the
deaths. These people from Reverend Carl's church don't know exactly
where he is or how to contact him."

"Did you find the other little girl?" John asked.

The medic shook his head sadly. "No," he said, "but we have people searching for her."

John nodded. "I understand," he said. "Please come in."

Mavis stepped passed the medic and embraced him. Through a flood of tears, she sobbed out her shock, grief, and confusion. Her husband was there, too, with his arms around them both. The disconsolate medic behind them suffered the same sorrows. He chewed his lip and waited until John turned and said, "Please come in."

For some minutes only tears were shed for the tornado's victims. But more pressing matters demanded attention. Nothing could be done for the unfortunate dead. The unfortunate survivors, as yet unaware of their loss, were still to suffer the terrible news.

"Carl and his step-father are in Nashville attending a church conference," Meg quavered. "Vernalee and Angela had the details, but those will be lost in the storm, I think. I don't know how you will find them."

"Will Angela's El Reno church know?" Mavis asked.

"I think so," Meg sniffed. "But with their pastor gone, no one will likely be there to take the call unless the assistant pastor is there."

"Do you have the number, Meg?"

"No, but you can get it from the operator. Just explain the nature of the problem, and she will find you someone to talk to."

And the operator did. The assistant pastor took her call and relayed the message to the Baptist Convention Center in Nashville. It was as cautious as it was sorrowful. He suggested that someone in charge should call him back and get the details. "We have survivors who are as much the victims of the storm as the actual casualties," he warned. "The news of the deaths must be delivered as gently as possible in the chapel or conference sanctuary. Please give them all the help and support you can. They will need it!"

Chapter 15

If one may choose the site for receiving tragic news, a religious setting might be the one of choice. Of course, tragic news is neither delivered nor received by choice but by expediency. It would seem that time is of the essence and that shock and grief can be alleviated somehow by getting the message to the unfortunate recipients as quickly as possible. That is not always true. The shocking results of the incomprehensible tragedy that had occurred two states away, only a few hours earlier, could not be eased by any speedy delivery.

The chairman of the conference that morning paused to read the written note handed to him. He whispered a question, listened, and turned his solemn face to peer at the large assemblage before him. His voice was grave. "I must excuse myself to make a phone call," he said. "It will take a few minutes. Please bear with me."

He returned some minutes later and again addressed the assemblage. He appeared stricken. "We have received news of an unfortunate tragedy that has occurred early this morning," he said. "The nature of that tragedy makes it necessary for me to recess this meeting for the present. Will all of our brothers and sisters be patient and wait until we can deliver that news to the parties involved? I would ask that brothers Bill Holmes, Ben Phillips, Robert Haynes, and Carl Claiborne come with me to the building chapel. The details of this tragic event will be revealed when we return. Please remain seated. Your assistance may be needed later." Solemnly, he led the four men to the nearest exit as the puzzled conferees watched them go.

Carl and his stepfather, aware of the singular significance of their relationship, instinctively knew that something bad was about to be revealed to them. The other two men had names on the conference program as people with considerable experience in counseling. Robert

Haynes immediately thought of his two daughters in El Reno and wondered. Carl Claiborne thought of his aging grandparents in Chisholm, alone and needing his help. The two counselors had their own private thoughts, as they all made their way to the quiet dimly lit chapel. Motioning to a tier of seats fronting the altar, the chairman said quietly, "Please sit down."

His whole demeanor was grave. His hands clasped together on his chest, his eyes pained and unblinking, the muscles of his cheeks bunched and twitching, all begged for mercy and understanding.

"I have just talked to a pastor in El Reno, Oklahoma," he said. "A tornado struck the little town of Chisholm about 5:00 o'clock this morning. Most of the town was spared, but four people died in the parsonage of a church...." His words were cut short by gasps, agonized wails, and the near collapse of Robert Haynes and his stepson. For some moments, they could barely survive the mental shock as they clung to each other and moaned. The stunned counselors moved quickly to their sides and held their trembling bodies. The bearer of the bad news looked above the altar at the icon of Christ on the cross and cried out, "Dear Christ, help us in this hour of need. Help us to understand this tragic loss of our brothers' loved ones. Help us to under stand, dear God!"

And from the lips of His devout follower, Carl Claiborne, he heard not a prayer but an accusation, "Dear God why have you forsaken me?" Then, he pitched forward and fell unconscious on the chapel floor.

Even the counselors were stricken. Desperately, they lifted him to a sitting position and checked for vital signs. They found his pulse rapid and irregular, his breathing labored and erratic. One rose and raced back to the conference hall and called for assistance. In seconds, a physician was in the chapel with his ever-present medical bag. He made a quick appraisal. His diagnosis was terse. "Severe shock bordering on cardiac arrest. Get both of these men to a hospital."

The two pastors spent the next several days in the hospital where sedatives and medical technology strove to ease the shock and trauma of their hurt minds. Their confused hearts resumed their faithful beating even though the minds continued to agonize over the reality of such a tragedy. And each day the counselors came to empathize with the two men and to soothe the hurt minds as best they could.

For Robert Haynes, they were helpful. He had spent most of his life rationalizing the inconsistencies in his religion. The reasons for the love of God, on the one hand, and his apparent cruelty on the other, he was hearing again from the counselors. "God's love is due to the nature of God himself," they said. "He does love humanity. After all, he gave his only begotten son to save humanity from its own evils. As for the ills of humankind, Satan is the cause of those."

"Why?" Carl wailed angrily, "Why does God permit that to happen?"

"Satan," the counselors said emphatically, "cannot bear to see humans happy. Those who are happiest he often tries to destroy. We believe that to be true in your tragedy. We can give no other explanation."

John Haynes felt the hurt in his heart ease slightly. The force that had destroyed his beloved wife, daughter-in-law, and grandchildren he could continue to hate. He need not feel guilty about being angry with his God, for God had no part in the tragic death of Angela, Vernalee, and the two innocent children. His hate for Satan he could keep in his heart and soul, even as the sorrow for his lost wife and grandchildren was permitted to drain slowly away. That he could deal with.

But for Carl, the counselor's explanation only added to his confusion. The incomprehensible and senseless deaths of his mother, wife, and children could not be rationalized in such a fashion. He had always taken seriously the Judo-Christian tenet that God was all-powerful. Had not God Himself said to Moses, "Thou shalt have none other gods before me!" And had he not also said, "Thou shalt not bow down thyself unto them, nor serve them." And, yet, he was hearing now the implication that God was not all-powerful and all-knowing, and that He had a rival god Who often challenged his authority. And God, who was said to be so all-knowing that he knew even "the fall of the sparrow," did not know something as large and awful as a killer tornado! That thought then switched his mind back to a vision of the tornado and to his beautiful family being victims of its destructive evil. His tears were unloosened again, and he turned his face away and wept. The counselor at his side could only lay his hand upon his sobbing form and wait.

When his grief spasms had passed, he dared to watch the ragged remnants of clouds through his second floor window. Perhaps, they had only a few hours earlier been spun off from the tornado. He wanted to curse them and accuse them of their part in death of his family. But they looked innocent enough and guiltless of any wrong. Perhaps, they had nothing to do with the tornado. Perhaps, like him, they were only innocent bystanders in a drama that even God could not direct. *If humans cannot rely on God,* he thought, *what can they rely on?* The futility of his devotion to God at that moment became enormous to him, and he wished that God would send a lightning bolt to destroy him as He had his family. His misery could then end, and an angel of God would reunite him with those whom He had so recently destroyed. "I would pray to God for that," he said to the counselor, "but he wouldn't be listening." And the counselor had gasped and turned away.

The hospital dismissed Robert Haynes the second day. "I need to go home," he said to Carl. "Your sisters need me. Funeral arrangements need to be made. I need to go, Carl. Will you be all right without me?"

"I will never be all right again," Carl mumbled. "But I understand your need to go. The attending physician has checked my physical condition and found nothing physically wrong with me but the mental shock. He says little else can be done for me except the proper sedatives to get me past this period of grief. So, go this afternoon. They need you there more than I need you here."

"I spoke on the phone with your grandmother this morning," his stepfather said. "Searchers found little Megan's body yesterday. I thought you would want to know."

After a long moment of silence Carl sniffed. "I take little comfort in that," he gritted. "It was the least decent thing God could do. Now, He flaunts his power to remind me of how frail humans really are. I will not thank him for that!"

Reverend Haynes gasped. "Oh, dear God," he moaned, "help this poor tortured soul to know Thy purpose!" For some moments he wept and babbled. Regaining a bit of composure, he pleaded, "Try, Carl, to accept God's will. It is your only hope now! It is too late for our lost loved ones. But we must go on. You need to understand that, if not for yourself, then for all of the others who are suffering too. They are all so very worried about you. Your grandmother wept when she told me."

Thoughts of his beloved grandmother weeping out the sorrowful news of his baby daughter being found softened Carl. "I'm sorry," he sobbed. "I want to go home, too."

"Your grandparents have promised to pick you up at the airport," his stepfather quavered. "They will keep in touch with the hospital about when you will be released. The counselor will see that you get on the plane."

His voice broke and for a moment it appeared as if he might lose control again. After a moment of silence, he took a deep breath and continued. "My prayers will be with you, Carl. Please, pray for all of us if you cannot pray for yourself. Life must go on, and prayer will help."

Carl's response was only a slow stony nod, "I will do what I can," he muttered.

Before Reverend Haynes' departure, the doctor warned him privately, "He will need watching. I sense a kind of despair that might be suicidal. He will need a strong support group to help him get through the funerals and the grieving."

"We all will," the pastor said. "But, God willing, we will all survive to see better times."

"I hope so," the doctor said.

Chapter 16

Carl was permitted to go home the following day. The counselor escorted him to the airport and remained to see him safely on the boarding ramp. In a daze, he walked woodenly through the ramp and stood before the plane's open door. The hostess, seeing his confusion, checked his passenger slip and escorted him to a window seat. There he sat the entire trip, scarcely aware of those around him.

Most of that time he spent staring out the small window in a dream-like state that was half fantasy and half reality. Only when he emerged from the passenger ramp to see his grandparents anxiously waiting for him did full reality come again. Their presence was reminiscence of home, and home was where the tornado had come to destroy those who had been so dear to him. Weeping uncontrollably, he was embraced lovingly by the only two people still alive who had seen the tragic storm. They led him directly to their parked car, and while John was retrieving his luggage, he and his loving grandmother wept out their mutual grief.

Seeing his grandparents helped to clear his dazed mind. He began asking questions, halting at first, but more pointed and rational, as they drove the thirty miles to El Reno. "Do you want to stop in El Reno?" John asked.

"I don't care," he replied.

John hesitated to ask the question. "I thought you might want to go to the mortuary," he said at last.

"No, I don't want to go," Carl said almost as if he was talking about the weather. His grandmother looked pained. Tears welled up in her eyes. "Why, Carl? Why don't you want to go?" she quavered.

"That would be the final proof that they are dead," he said very softly. "I don't think that I am ready to believe that." His words trailed off into a series of sniffs and sighs as he stared out the window at the passing traffic.

"That will be all right, Carl" John assured him. "We will stop at your family's house, though. You must not forget that you have two sisters who need you. They are suffering, too, and are looking to their brother for support and comfort."

"Yes," Carl sighed. "I have not given them much thought. Now, I wonder how they were able to suffer through this."

"They have had relatives and their church," John reminded him. "But their loss is the same as yours. The same loved ones you grieve for, they also grieve for. Their grief can be no less than your grief. You must remember that."

"Did they pray for the safety of their mother?"

"I don't know, Carl."

"I did. That morning when we left I prayed for them all. And a few hours later, God took them all away. He took Mama, and he took Vernalee. He even took my innocent babies, leaving the little one to die alone in the darkness. I will never trust God again."

"Don't say that, Carl," his grandmother pleaded. "God didn't destroy your family! The tornado did."

"And God couldn't stop it?" Carl demanded angrily.

"I don't know," Meg whimpered.

John slowed, pulled onto a side street, and stopped. He looked back at the two in the rear seat and his voice was severe. "When we get home we will talk about that, Carl. Please don't hurt your grandmother more. She is suffering, too. We all are! But there are reasons why these things happen, and you won't find them in your religion. Quit believing that you have been betrayed! Quit believing that this pain is yours only. Please Carl, don't make it so hard for the rest of us!"

His grandfather's words were like ice water pouring over him. He was shocked awake and the confusion in his mind was suddenly eased. For the first time since he was given the tragic news he sensed hope. Unaccountably, he knew that he could trust his grandfather more than any person alive to help him find his way out of the nightmare he was suffering. He took a deep breath and quavered,

"I'm sorry! I have not meant to be so self-centered. But I have lost everything!"

"No, Carl, not quite everything. You still have your sisters and stepfather. And you have your grandmother and me. And above all you have your sanity if you choose to save it. You can only do that by facing the reality of what has happened."

Carl shuddered and choked off a sob. "How do I do that? Oh, God!" he wailed. "How do I do that?"

"You must go with us to the mortuary," Meg said urgently. "You must, Carl!"

"And you must stiffen yourself," John gritted. "It is not grief alone that destroys the human spirit. It is cold unrelenting despair! Grow angry, if you must! Curse the tornado! Rail at Fate! Defy, if you wish, the God who you think has betrayed you. Then, accept all the love and understanding that will flow your way from the rest of us. We will be there for you, Carl." Grimly, he returned to their route of travel and proceeded to the Baptist parsonage.

The reunion with his sisters and stepfather was very emotional. Had he not remembered his grandfather's words, he surely could not have survived it. *"Stiffen yourself,"* his grandfather had said, and he did. Later, when he stood before the four coffins, he heard himself muttering, "Goddamn the tornado!" And he lay his trembling hand on each of the lifeless faces and murmured, "God has betrayed us. If I cannot understand His reasons, I will never trust Him again!" Then he moved as a blind man to a chair against the far wall and stared into a blank nothingness. He was strangely calm when his sisters followed him there and sat beside him.

"Carl?" the older one queried. "Are you all right?"

"I want to go home, now," he said. "I have no more grief to give."

"Will you stay with us tonight," his sister asked.

"My grandparents need me," he said quietly. "I will go home with them."

"Will we see you again before the funeral services?"

"No," he said, "I am very tired. It will be best if I have some time to myself. I need to think. I need to find my way out of this. Please explain to Papa. He will understand. I hope that my sisters will, too."

"Yes, of course," they said tearfully. "We know your hurt, for it is also our hurt."

It was also John's hurt and Meg's hurt, and not since the time they had stood by their son's casket in Las Vegas twenty-two years earlier had they been so devastated. But now, they had seen the threat to their grandson's sanity turned away and were encouraged. Meg observed, "You are right, John. The bad times do follow the good times. Tell me, then, do the good times come back to follow the bad ones?"

"Of course!" he asserted. "How else could humans survive?"

Meg gave his arm a gentle squeeze and smiled wistfully. For her, the crisis had passed.

The multiple funeral, two days later, would bring to a close the week's tragic event. The week had begun on a happy note the past Monday morning. Less than twenty-four hours later, the tornado had struck to claim four innocent victims whose awareness of self and all things earthly were quickly erased. By mid-morning on Tuesday, Carl, his stepfather, and two sisters became the tornado's secondary victims. But for the secondary victims, the pain was not quickly over. It could never be over. It could only be diminished by the passing of time with happier days to act as sedatives to ease the anguish lingering from that tragic week. In that sense, the good times alone do not always follow the bad. Sometimes the bad ones manage to trail along like unwelcome mongrel dogs following their former masters, who are to be continually reminded of their presence. Humans can never be completely rid of disaster or the memories of disaster.

Chapter 17

The funeral service for the four victims of the tornado's fury was unprecedented. Never in its eighty-year history had the Hosanna Baptist Church been called on to bury four of its own who had died violently from what some had called the "Wrath of God." The news media had been especially attentive to the story from the earliest moment when, in the dawn of that previous Tuesday morning, the small town of Chisholm, Oklahoma had lost its church parsonage and the family of its much loved young minister. Though spring tornadoes were not uncommon in their part of the world, for one to strike God's own institution with such tragic consequences was appalling. People found themselves pondering their faith and the unaccountable anger of their God. The question on most everyone's lips and minds was, "Why?"

Even the solemn, sad-eyed mourners at the service that following Monday afternoon spoke the question silently. It was in their downcast eyes and in the almost imperceptible wagging of their bowed heads as they stared unseeing at the backs of the pews in front of them. A half dozen journalists from throughout the state, having made themselves as unobtrusive as possible, saw and heard the question over and over again as they mingled with the stricken citizens of Canadian County. And the most confused and stricken of that huge assembly were the chief mourners on the two front rows reserved for them. Numbed by the unexplainable tragedy, they chose to dwell on the question and to ignore the visiting minister's words of condolence and promise of eternal life.

But the minister spoke the question, too, for it was also on his mind. "No one can know why this has happened," he said. "God's ways are often secretive and mysterious, but He surely must have his reasons. We can only take comfort in the thought that our lot is not to question why but to be persistent in our faith in Him and wait for Judgment Day when these things will be revealed to us."

And for John and Meg Claiborne, sitting in the second row a dozen feet below him, the futility of the minister's platitudes only increased their sense of urgency. Carl, at their side, took a deep breath and let it out again, almost as if he had expected some revelation to clarify his confusion. Out of the corners of their eyes, Meg and John saw his mouth tighten and his jaw muscles harden. The minister's words had not helped their grandson! Help for him could not wait for Judgment Day. He needed it now, and it could only come from them. How that could be, Meg did not know, but John did.

He had thought long and hard the past week about the dilemma facing the people of faith. For them, the minister's words must suffice. They were words of resignation, for no other explanation was possible within the bounds of their faith. Cold hard reality about humanity's real nature and its true place in the world could not coexist with that faith. Carl would have to see his world through other windows. He must walk through other doors. And John knew that he must do it alone. *I can point the way,* he thought, *but he must make the journey.*

The four caskets were opened for a final viewing, and after much weeping and wringing of hands, they were closed again and borne by solemn pallbearers to waiting hearses. A funeral procession stretching endlessly through the quiet town followed them at last to the municipal cemetery where they were interred as a family group. The cluster of four graves would serve forever as a sad reminder of the tornado's perfidy.

Though the funeral service was done and over, the sad ordeal would be a long time in the hearts and minds of Oklahoma citizens. It would be forever in the memories of friends and survivors of the unfortunate victims. In the annals of Canadian County, it would be a part of its history. For Carl Claiborne, it was also to shape his destiny.

But he did not know that, as he turned to look one last time at the workers closing the graves. Nor did he seem to be very aware of anything. Life held an ideal past, a cruel present, and a bitter future for him. He wanted to shut it out. He wanted it to go away! More than anything, he wished to die and be free from his torment and pain. In the rear seat of his grandparent's car, he huddled in the embrace of his grandmother, and wept like a despairing child. Meg could do nothing but weep with him. And John could only stare grimly at the road ahead and plan his strategy for turning tragedy into a kind of triumph. *I must begin immediately,* he said. *Meg will give him the sedatives the doctors have proscribed, and he will sleep through the night. Tomorrow, when he is more stable, we will begin our talks.*

That evening, Carl nibbled at his food and ate little. Throughout the entire week of his ordeal he had taken little nourishment, and Meg had watched his usual robust form slowly shrink away. In desperation, she offered him a bowl of warm milk and two slices of buttered toast. Seeing her concern, he smiled for the first time that day and ate it all.

"I am sorry, Grandmother," he apologized. "You are so good to me, and I have been such a trial to you. But tomorrow, I will do better."

"We will all do better," she murmured. "I will draw you a warm bath, if you wish. It will help you relax for a good night's rest. In the morning, I will expect you to eat a good breakfast so that we can begin again."

"Sausage and eggs?" he asked.

"Whatever you want, Carl, and whenever you want it," she promised, smiling.

"I'll plan on that," her grandson said. He looked across the table at John and said quietly, "We will have breakfast, Grandpa, and then we can have the talks that you spoke about. I want to see the church. We will need to decide what to do with it."

"We will do that," Grandpa said.

Chapter 18

Only scattered evidence of the previous week's storm remained on the day after the funerals. Clean-up crews had been eager to erase as much as they could, and parishioners had made hasty repairs to the damaged church. The insurance company had authorized funds to replace the missing windows with clear panes.

"Later," they had said, "if it is the wish of the church to have stained replacement windows, we can make the change. For now, we must protect the interior from future rains."

"And the roof?" John Claiborne had asked, "What can we do about that?"

"We can make temporary repairs," they had said. "The steeple needs to be stabilized now to prevent it from falling and injuring workers below. We will likely need to remove it completely to close up and seal the roof."

"Do that now," John said. "We have no idea about the future of this church. Both its heart and soul have been destroyed. Its future fate will determine the nature of the final repairs."

And its fate was to be in the balance that morning as John led Carl through the church grounds. There, children had once played while their parents picnicked and relaxed on Sunday afternoons. But it was not a picnic area any longer. The young trees and shrubbery had not survived the violent winds that had rampaged through one week earlier. Most were uprooted or broken and reduced to splinters to be scattered by the storm's fury.

Carl surveyed the area glumly. "The Wrath of God!" he muttered.

"No," John corrected him, "the Wrath of Nature. That is what we must talk about. But you should see the other damage first. I know that you will find it painful, but you must also see the parsonage. Only in that way can you get closure to what has happened. Then the healing can begin."

They detoured around the church where repair crews were already beginning their work. When the hulk of the once lovely parsonage came into view, Carl took one look and turned away. "Oh, dear God!" he groaned. For a long moment, he stood looking at he ground as he fought to control himself.

His grandfather lay his hand across his shoulders and whispered, "It's all right to grieve, Carl. I understand your pain. But it is absolutely necessary that you face the reality of this enemy that is destroying you. Let me show you the track it followed to come here." He turned his grandson away from the ruined parsonage and led him to the gaping hole at the western end of the line of cedar trees.

"It came from there," he said, pointing toward the southwest. "It leveled the vacant house, barn, and a small grove of locust trees where the Wilhelms once lived. You can see the path it took through the wheat fields and across the fence rows as it wandered haphazardly to get here. It was a mindless mass of energy that had no other purpose than to spend itself. You must believe me, Carl! It was not God that destroyed your family, it was Nature—blind, mindless, unguided Nature."

"Otherwise known as the Wrath of God," Carl reminded him grimly.

"Some people call it that," John admitted. "But that is because they have no other way to identify it. And that is your problem, Carl. That is what we need to discuss. Many people simply do not know about the real world. They confuse it with Biblical rhetoric, and the two become a confused conglomeration of fact and fancy. The good things of this world are attributed to God, and the bad things are equally divided between God and Satan. Humans haven't yet learned who they are, so they cannot understand that they are a part of the world of Nature. Many have yet to learn that they, like all the other creatures on this earth, are subject to its whims and random acts. Doesn't that make sense, Carl?"

"It is not what I have been taught," Carl muttered. "The Bible teaches that the bad things of the earth are because of Adam and

Eve's disobedience to God. They ate of the tree of knowledge and mankind is still being punished for that original sin."

John spat at the ground. "I want to think about that," he said. "But we have stood in this one spot long enough. We need to find a comfortable place in the shade where we can relax and consider all these thing that you have been taught and all these things I have studied and observed in my seventy-seven years." He looked to the east and pointed to the seventy-one year old cedar tree he had help his father plant just before he was to begin his first year of school. He had trimmed its lower branches and placed in its shade a picnic table with comfortable benches for times when he wanted to relax while the new town was being built. Meg had often met him there at noontime with a basket of drinks and food, and they had chatted and lazed an hour or so away. After a cooling drink, a sandwich or two, and a quiet nap in a lounge chair, he had usually gone back to his work rested and refreshed. It was a good place with good memories. It would be a good place to talk.

He looked at his watch and was surprised to see that the morning was almost gone. *No matter,* he thought. *Time is of no consequence today. I have things to do.*

Together, they walked slowly through the May morning past the old farmhouse of his youth, one wise in years and eager to teach, the other confused and hoping for the wisdom to understand. As they strolled along, John explained how the long line of trees had come to be. "Each represents a year of my life in the public schools," he said. "I learned many things there. Some have proved valuable to me, and I cherish them. Others were trite and impractical. Many of them I forgot or threw away. It is that way with learning. We have to look through a lot of chaff to find the kernels of truth."

Carl found that to be a bit droll, and he uttered a soft two-syllable chuckle. It was his first response to humor in his long difficult week. "That sounds almost Biblical, Grandpa," he mused. "How can you tell which is truth and which is chaff?"

"I admit that I often do not know what truth is," Grandpa said, "but I can usually recognize what truth isn't. I also have learned that truth is primarily a human concept. We are the only creatures that seem to consider it very important. I suppose that might be because of our intelligence. It has provided a very fertile field for our curiosities, and they have sprouted and grown like weeds in a cornfield. We want to know everything, and mostly, we want to know 'Why'. 'What, when, where, how' all lead to that ultimate puzzling question, 'Why?' If that question cannot be answered quickly and easily, we begin inventing theories that soon become answers, some right and some wrong. The wrong answers are often based on appearances or how we imagine or want things to be. But eventually, they are proved to be untrue even though the real truth may remain undetermined."

Carl took a seat on the picnic table and pondered his grandfather's words. His face was solemn again as he studied the older man's face. "Are you trying to tell me that God had nothing to do with the death of my mother and family?" he asked.

"Yes, Carl, I am saying that for the third time. Please believe me! You can never have peace until you accept that."

"Then why have things like that so often been called 'the wrath of God?'" Carl gritted.

"Because people demand answers!" John emphasized. "For thousands of years they have endured earthquakes, fires, floods, and all kinds of natural disasters. Pestilence, disease, famine—you name it. People have suffered and died for reasons unknown to them. They could not know or understand that this world is a chaotic place of conflicting energies that need to be vented. If puny humans get in the way of those energies, they suffer and die like all other creatures, and no God, real or imagined, can be prevailed on to interfere. But humans in their arrogance believe that they have a favored place on this earth and deserve special protection from their God. They keep inventing answers to their questions, 'Why?'"

"How do you know this, Grandpa?" Carl asked, with a tinge of suspicion coloring his question.

"Because every culture has come up with answers different from those in other cultures. They seldom have logic and practicality. What is one culture's religion is another culture's myths and superstitions."

"And do you think Christianity is one of those?" A bit of scorn had crept into the question.

"If I were a Muslim, I would think so," John said. "Muslims are even more devoted to their beliefs than most Christians. Why should Christians begrudge them a place in God's world?"

Shocked out of his lethargy, Carl was aghast. "You are a Muslim, Granddad?" he asked.

His grandfather chuckled. Secretly, he was pleased to see the awakened state of his grandson. That meant that his mind was being receptive to things other that the week's tragic events. "No, of course not," he said. "Nor am I Hindu, Buddist, Shinto, or any of the many other belief systems scattered around the globe. I am a free thinker who believes that logic and reasoning are the only ways to resolve the questions about who we are and how we can best deal with the natural world. That may have been what the ancients meant by the 'tree of knowledge', Genesis 2, verse 17. It is one of the few Biblical passages I can quote. It says, 'But of the tree of the knowledge of good and evil, thou shalt not eat of it: for in the day that thou eatest thereof thou shalt surely die.' That seems to indicate that the ancient scribes wanted to keep their followers ignorant."

"Then you are a sinner, Grandpa!"

"Perhaps I am in the eyes of those who live by those words. But sin is also a human concept. If denying the right to the knowledge of one's world promotes ignorance, which is the greater sin, knowledge, or ignorance? How much do you know about the earth sciences, Carl?"

"I have been told that too much science poisons the mind, Grandpa, so I haven't learned too much."

"It has been said that a little learning is a dangerous thing. Do you believe that, Carl?"

"Yes, if it is the wrong kind of learning."

"Would that include science? Did you take science in your Baptist high school?"

"I had general science."

"No biology, no chemistry, no geology?"

"We had all that in general science."

"Did you have any meteorology?"

"That was included in general science!" Carl sputtered. His voice now held exasperation with a tinge of anger.

Grandpa backed off. He saw a twenty-seven year old man beginning to resent a line of questioning that was dangerous to his self-image and beliefs. Further questioning would likely create a mindset against any revelation about why the tornado had claimed his family.

"I'm sorry, Carl," he said gently. "I didn't mean to be so nosy." He looked at his watch and in some surprise exclaimed, "Great Scott, it's almost 1:00 o'clock! Your Grandma will be wondering what has happened to us. Don't you think we had better get something to eat?"

Carl sighed and stood up. "I think we should, Grandpa," he replied.

Chapter 19

Meg was in the open doorway looking out when they came up the walk. "I was beginning to wonder about you two," she said with feigned severity. "I didn't quite know if or when I should fix lunch."

Remembering the good breakfast that he and Carl had finished earlier, John arched his brows and observed, "A hungry dog is a better hunter than a well fed one. We are still digesting the sausage and eggs we had this morning."

As they followed her through the back hallway and into the kitchen, she asked, "And what were you two dogs hunting that kept you out since breakfast?"

"We weren't hunting very hard, were we Carl?"

"It would seem that we were hunting Truth," Carl sniffed sorrowfully. "We saw what the tornado did, but I am still wondering why."

Meg's face softened. "Keep an open mind, Carl. And listen to your grandfather. He is wiser in many ways than some of us. I keep learning from him, and I really believe that you will, too."

Carl, misty eyed and solemn, said softly, "I will, Grandmother. I promise."

"While I am fixing lunch, you might like to look at some things that I found recently in several boxes of your father's things. We brought them with us when we came here to build our town, and they have been stored in a closet in the old house ever since. Last winter, on his fiftieth birthday, I got up the courage to see what was in them." She sighed and turned away to stare out a kitchen window.

John went to stand beside her. "I wish I had known," he murmured. "We could have done it together."

"I know how emotional you get," she explained. "You had gone to a town meeting, and I was feeling down. So I brought them here and spent the afternoon reminiscing."

"And crying some, too, I would guess."

"A little," Meg admitted, "but it was good for me. There were enough good memories to ease the hurt. You and Carl should go through the things. I found that helpful when I did. I think you will, too."

Carl was solemn. "I would like to do that, Grandmother. I know so little about my father. And I have needed him so many times, especially now. Perhaps, I can draw strength from seeing and touching something that was once his."

"Where are the boxes, Meg?" John asked. "I think they may be what we both need at this moment."

"They're on the floor in the back of our walk-in closet. You will find them heavy. I had to unload them and make several trips to get them all over here."

"I could have helped you, Meg," John scolded. "But never mind! Carl and I can manage them together."

"Bring them down to the library. Then we'll decide what to do with everything later," Meg said.

They were indeed heavy, but as John had said they were manageable, and they soon had them stacked in a corner of the small library. "I remember that some of them contain his books," he said. "They were labeled somewhere on the side."

"It says 'Clothing' on this one. Why would Grandma want to keep that?"

"He had some of his favorite things," John mused. "Fraternity sweaters, crazy hats, ties, and the like. I think they may have meant more to his mother than to him. Empty it out on the couch, and we'll take a look."

John was right, and one by one, Carl held each in his two hands as he studied solemnly what had once been his father's very personal and private possessions. "It is so hard for me to picture him wearing these," he said, "but I do remember the photographs Grandmother showed me when I came here the first few times. I remember the college look of the clothes. Was he a good student, Grandpa?"

John nodded and for a few moments remained lost in his own thoughts. Then he took a deep breath and let it out again. He pointed to the bottom box and said, "That one will have his books, essay assignments, and grade reports. Meg kept them all. She was a proud mother, and he was a proud loving son." He lifted away the other boxes and opened the one that bore the caption, "Frank's College Papers & Books."

Carl bit his lower lip and lifted one out. But it was not a college text but an old faded blue volume titled EUCLID'S PRINCIPALS OF PLANE GEOMETRY. John took one look and gasped. "Good grief!" he muttered, "that's the old text book I used when I was in high school! I had no idea it still existed. I'll have to ask Meg about that. I'll bet she found it in the attic of that old house. Now, I suppose that you will ask me if I was a good student?" He chuckled and looked owlishly at his grandson.

"Were you, Grandpa?"

"That was my favorite class in my sophomore year at Bridgeport High," Grandpa declared. "It changed me from being an average student to being one who made all the honor rolls."

Carl looked at the older man with a bit of skepticism, and for a moment he was transported from his week of tragedy to a much different and simpler time when there were none of the trappings of his own time. Puzzled, he asked, "How could that one class change you that much?"

"It taught me how to think," John said. "Until then, I had been a receiver of information. Like a baby bird in the nest, I dutifully gulped down whatever the teachers poked at me. I never doubted their words, I never asked why. If they said '*i before e, except after c*', I followed the rule and spelled according to that rule. If they said, '*invert the divisor and multiply*', I did that. I didn't ask why, I didn't care why. I just did it. Of course, I did wonder sometimes why the teachers marked my spelling words wrong when they should have been right. Take the word, 'thief' for instance. It is spelled according to the rule and is correct. But what about 'height', or 'heifer', and 'science', for instance, or 'leisure'? When I spelled them, I wrote '*hieght*', '*hiefer*', and '*sceince*', just like the rule said, and they were marked wrong. So were '*fient*' and '*biege*', and '*liesure*', and to this day I am never quite sure how to spell those words."

"I guess there are exceptions to the rule," Carl suggested.

"It seems to so," Grandpa agreed, "But not in geometry! If an axiom says, 'The shortest distance between two points is a straight line', it is true, always true, and without exceptions. I liked that. Euclid set forth his mathematical laws according to the way they are in pure logic and nature, and two thousand years later, they are still as infallible as then. That class taught me how to reason and arrive at a logical result—if there is one, of course—and every since I have based my thinking on that premise."

"Oh, shit!" Carl exclaimed, "you said that Nature did not play by the rules. The damn tornado didn't!"

"It played according to the rules of meteorological science and physics, but you must understand those rules," John scolded. He turned his attention back to the box and removed another book. "Hmmn," he mused. But he quickly laid it aside and turned to study his grandson whose angry outburst of earthy language had startled him. He stopped his musings and peered over his spectacles at Carl. "When did you start using that kind of language?" he asked.

"Since you told me to get angry if I needed to. Well, I need to! I'm tired of being the nice religious pastor whose family was brutalized by an uncaring God. There, I've said it!"

"Does it make you feel better now that you've said it?"

"Sure as Hell, it does!"

John grinned. "Then do it more often," he exclaimed. "Emotions that are not released can be poison. They burn out the guts and shrivel hope. We all need to get angry when we suffer tragedies like last week."

"So you keep saying that! How can I really believe it?" Carl's voice was grim and challenging.

John took a deep breath and let it out again. "You've asked an honest question, Carl, and you are entitled to an honest answer. You are privileged to accept what I say or to reject it. I only ask that you give it some thought. Are you prepared to consider other possibilities about your problem? It's all about understanding, and it didn't just happen suddenly. It's been building up since you were born. Through no fault of your own, you have seen your world and your God through narrow stained glass windows. The real world and the real God have escaped you and many others like you. You have been taught to believe what others have wanted you to believe."

But Carl's anger did not go away. It was only magnified. He was aghast. "How can you say that? I believe what most people believe. Godalmighty, Grandpa, how can you say that?"

"Because many people have come to doubt it. They no longer believe in the Genesis version of creation. Science has disproved that in so many ways that it now becomes laughable. Were you ordained to believe it, Carl, or did you swallow it all like I swallowed some of the rules in grade school?"

"I've always believed it! My mother believed it! My church believes it now! Why shouldn't I believe it!"

"Because it has led you to misidentify the God who you think has betrayed you. I'm sorry, Carl, but you asked, and it's the only answer I can give."

Carl shrugged. His voice turned surly. "Well, you said I didn't have to believe you, so I won't. I'll just have another look at my father's stuff."

"You could do that at your leisure when you're not upset." John said. "I remember that the books are well marked with his notes and comments. They should give you some notion of who your father was. They also may give you an idea of the kind of troubles your mother and he were having when he died. And, Carl, maybe they will give you a reason to reconsider your philosophies about life. Maybe they will make you want to go back to school again."

"Why? I am twenty-seven years old. No one ever goes back to school at my age. What good would that do?"

"What will you do if you don't? You want answers. Can you return to your work in the church without the satisfaction of having those answers? Do you feel prepared to take up some other line of work?"

Carl stared at his grandfather. His reply was almost sullen. "I don't know, Granddad. I just don't know."

"I understand, Carl. I really do, and I know it will take a while for you to figure it out. A lot of soul searching will be needed. Only you can do that, but other viewpoints can help. Take, for instance, this book of your father's, *'Introduction to Historical Geology'*." He leafed through it and noted the penciled notes along the margins and the numerous underscored passages that his young son had once considered important. "A lot of important ideas are in here, and you should take a look at them. Your father was very smart, Carl. You can learn from this book as he did. Then the idea of returning to school may not seem so strange." Handing the book to Carl, he added, "Now, I think we should go down and see what your grandma has fixed for two hungry hunting dogs."

Carl was not listening. He was already intent on examining the old college textbook and the whispered notations of a father almost unknown to him. For the next two days, it was to be rarely out of his hands. His transition had begun.

Chapter 20

Carl studied his father's old textbook far into the night. He paid special attention to the notes and comments neatly penciled in the margins. They usually had reference to underlined portions that once had special meaning to the shadowy figure who had been his father. The very first one of those was in the introduction, the part of a textbook most often ignored by ordinary students. But Frank Claiborne apparently had not been ordinary. He had wanted to know what the book was all about before committing his time and energies toward learning its contents. The author had clearly stated his philosophy, and the underlined portion immediately caught Carl's eye. It stated:

> "—To think accurately and to analyze soundly any set of observations are abilities far more valuable to a student than the capacity for repeating something read or heard by him. Memory is useful as an adjunct to learning but not a substitute for real learning."

An accompanying notation penciled in the margin made Carl smile. *"My father has said that many times!"* it stated. The words were different, but their meaning was the same as what Carl had heard that father, now his own grandfather, express only hours before. *Gramps might be right,* he thought ruefully. *Maybe, all I think I know is just hearsay fed to me by parent birds who were fed earlier in the same way!* The notion settled deep in his gut and would not go away. It was to dominate his thinking throughout the time he was to spend trying to understand the textbook's contents.

He could not understand some of it. Though its contents were basically simple, he had difficulty with many words and phrases that were new to him. The notations helped, but he came to realize that his lack of a background in high school science would make it

117

impossible for him to know fully what his father had apparently mastered rather easily. He began to feel intellectually inadequate, and dual feelings of ignorance and guilt also settled in his gut to mingle with that earlier notion.

Evolution had been one of the most reviled concepts through his years of religious training, and its ugly face was kept hidden from him and other young and receptive minds. It was considered to be blasphemy of all things sacred, for its claims directly threatened Old Testament truths that were the underpinnings of all Christian philosophy. Built brick by brick, generation by generation, over a thousand years of Jewish history, that citadel could crumble if those truths were ever shown to be false. The institution of Christianity would then become suspect and fall into decay.

He found that almost as frightening as the loss of faith in his God, and he put the book aside and attempted to divert his thinking by taking long walks along the animal trails through the wildlife refuge outside the town. But that only gave rise to questions about the nature of life and how it had became so varied. The ugly face of evolution would not go away. Invariably, he would return to his room, take up the book and consider the possibility of evolution.

The chapter on Nature and Evolution of Mesozoic Life was lengthy and graphic. He could not put its ideas out of his mind. He found himself becoming obsessed with them. He even found himself discussing them with his grandparents. At first, his purpose was to find support for his old creationist beliefs, but when he saw their cool reception to his ideas, he realized that they were, as John Claiborne had indicated earlier, actually strong believers of evolution.

"Too much evidence supports it, Carl," his grandfather asserted. "The fossil record shows without doubt that life forms have been changing for millions or even billions of years. Humans have only been here a million years or so. I don't understand how anyone can dispute the evidence."

"Millions of years, Grampa? How can anybody know that?"

"They can't know exactly, but by studying and analyzing the rock strata where the fossils are found, they are satisfied with their estimates."

Carl continued to be doubtful. He squinted at his grandfather and frowned. "If they know so much why can't they give us something more exact?"

"Would you prefer the theory of the English theologian who had it figured to the exact year?" Gramps asked. "I don't remember his name or the date of his calculation, but he had the age of the earth figured out to be a only about three or four thousand years. We don't hear much about him anymore because we know how impossible that is. Geologists with their millions or billions of years are more realistic than that. Their findings and how life has evolved are now facts of life."

Carl remained silent for a long time. He picked at his food and pondered his Grandfather's words. At last, he looked at his grandmother and asked, "What do you believe, Grandma? Do you believe that we came from monkeys?"

"Not really," she said, "but I do believe that we share a common ancestor somewhere in the dim past. The African fossils support the belief."

"It doesn't seem possible to me," Carl replied.

"Would you rather believe that Eve was created from Adam's rib?"

"I guess that seems unlikely, too." Carl admitted.

"It certainly does to me," Meg snipped. "I refuse to be thought of as a descendent of some man's rib. The creationists have no evidence to support their claims, Carl. The evolutionists have museums and universities loaded with fossil evidence."

John smiled wryly as he finished his piece of lemon pie. He laid down his fork and said rather smugly, "Hey, we have evidence in a small canyon less than a half-mile from here."

"Yes, of course, John," Meg broke in. "Why don't you show him what we have in our own backyard?"

Carl was suddenly alert. "Really, Grandpa?" he asked. "Or is this another one of your goofy jokes?"

"It's no joke!" Grandpa hastened to explain. "I haven't spread it around much, but when I was about fifteen, I was looking for arrow points in a narrow canyon west of here and discovered some sort of fossil that was not supposed to be there. Only a part of it was exposed in the gravel below the edge of a sandstone ledge, but it looked like a leg bone and was at least three or four feet long. I expect that it is still there if you want to help me find it."

"Can I go too?" Meg asked. "You have been promising to take me there for twenty years."

"If you feel that your aging system is up to it."

"My aging system has been jogging a mile and a half every morning before you are up! So what else do I need to get your permission?"

"Are you willing to help me in and out of the canyon?" her husband teased.

"Carl and I together can do that," Meg said tartly.

"When?" Carl asked. "This is Friday, and I haven't seen my El Reno family since—" and his voice broke to interrupt him. For some moments he wept silently. His grandparents quickly joined him and they all wept together. "I'm sorry," he said, wiping his eyes. "I can't bear the reality of what has happened. I try, but I continue to hurt inside." He sniffed and continued with words tearful and halting. "I need to see about buying a car. The tornado also took that away from me. I found it rolled up in the brushy draw below where the fence used to be."

"Do you want us to go with you?" Grandpa quavered.

"No, I may want to stay a few days. I know they will be wondering about me. If you don't mind, I'll drive your pickup truck."

"Take the car. It's clean and full of fuel," Grandpa insisted, "— and stay as long as you like. If you buy a car, let us know, and we'll pick ours up later."

"Call us," Grandmother murmured. "And we will go looking for Gramp's fossil when you get back."

Carl breathed a deep sorrowful sigh and nodded. "I will," he promised.

He spent the weekend with family and friends, and much of that time was quiet and meditative as they all tried to put the tragedy behind them. Sunday services were more solemn than usual with frequent references to the sad events that had befallen the Haynes family. The young assistant pastor, having distinguished himself very well during those trying days, continued to assume that role. His message was based on a familiar theme. "God never gives us a burden too great for us to bear," he said. "Whatever questions we may have about the reasons for those burdens, we can take comfort in the thought that His purpose will be revealed to us on Judgement Day. We must never forget that He loves us and is aware of our suffering."

And for the first time in his memory, Carl sat stonily silent when the "Amens" were murmured throughout the congregation. And he continued to dwell on the message, now punched full of holes by his doubts. Mixed with guilt, his thoughts were to plague him through the next several days. He found himself being noncommittal and unresponsive to his family's comments regarding the young minister's message. And his stepfather began to take notice. Never before had his stepson failed to show interest in their analysis of the Sunday morning services. They had frequently critiqued each other to draw attention to questionable comments, incorrect quotation of scripture, and manner of delivery. From the older minister, Carl had learned much.

And so had the young assistant minister who was to assume a church pastorate of his own in the days ahead. But Carl, continuing to ponder the many things he had been taught, kept returning to the words that his real father had underlined thirty years earlier in a geology textbook. Slowly, his doubts gelled into strong suspicions that those Biblical teachings had no real basis.

In his several years in the ministry, he had witnessed several instances in which God's burden, contrary to the old platitude, had been too heavy. He had known several despairing sufferers of life's trials who had resorted to suicide or other desperate acts. God did indeed give burdens too heavy to be borne by mortal men! If his grandparent had not urged him to get angry and resist despair, he himself would almost certainly have been one of them.

The other platitude about the truth being made known to us on Judgement Day is also questionable, he mused. *Who can honestly bear witness to that?* He dared to ask his stepfather that question.

The discussion that followed created waves shocking enough to destroy their unity of purpose. Robert Haynes, esteemed stepfather and mentor, and Carl Claiborne, his devoted stepson and disciple, became incompatible.

The older man's casual remark about their burden of sorrow triggered the discussion leading to their estrangement, and Carl had reminded him of the short prayer service they had held that Tuesday morning before their departure for the Nashville conference. "Why were our prayers not granted that day?" he asked. "We asked for God to care for them and to protect them. He did not! Instead he allowed them to be destroyed. I can never believe in him again until I know why!"

"Carl!" his stepfather exclaimed, "You surely can't mean that!"

"I do mean it! You tell me that God loves us! Yet, He behaves like a tyrant and refuses to reveal His reasons. I think I am entitled to know. I must know! Yesterday, Reverend Krantz said that God's reasons would be revealed to us on Judgement Day. Well, I can't wait that long. If God can't do that for me now, I will cease to believe he exists. I will begin to explore that possibility this fall when I enroll in a university. My grandparents are urging me to do that."

"Don't listen to them, Carl! Your place is in Chisholm with your church. The people need you. The church can be repaired."

"But can my faith be repaired?"

"Of course, Carl, but you must first accept what God has chosen to give you!"

And Carl's response was to astonish them both. It carried the bitter anger that his Grandfather had encouraged him to feel. "God has destroyed both my faith and my church!" he exclaimed. "So let him repair them! At such time as when He reveals himself to me, either through love or anger, I shall not be his servant!"

His stepfather was aghast. "That is blasphemy!" he sputtered.

"God will strike you dead for such thoughts."

"Let him! Then He can tell me why He destroyed my loyal loving family! If God is really listening, He can do it now. If He does not, you can begin to recognize as I have, that we do not know who or what God is."

"You cannot say that in this house," Robert Haynes shouted. "This is no longer your house! It is God's house, and I am telling you to leave it. May God have pity on your soul!"

"God's capacity for pity has already been demonstrated," Carl said calmly. "I will get my things and go. My thoughts will continue to be with you, if not my prayers. It will be my hope that the light of reason and truth will shine here in this house someday." He gathered his belongings and returned to Chisholm. The following day he and his grandparents went shopping in Oklahoma City for his new car.

Chapter 21

In the days ahead, Carl's grandparents recognized the changes in his behavior. His spates of grieving became less frequent and emotional. Though solemn and seriously thoughtful, his entire manner indicated that the times of agony, doubt, and dismay were passing. And at no time was it more evident than when the three of them went to investigate John's fossil discovery over a half century earlier.

"It may not be there anymore," Meg had suggested.

"If it's what I think it is," her husband replied, "Sixty years shouldn't make any difference."

"What do you think it might be, Gramps? A mastodon?" Carl asked eagerly.

John looked at him, and his quick surprise was almost comical. "Where did you get that idea?" he asked.

"From the geology book, Gramps. It said that mastodons and other elephants were common in North America before the last ice age."

"You're right. But I think what we are about to go and see is much older that that. It has too much sandstone above it. I may be wrong, but it might date back to late Mesozoic times."

"What does that mean, John?" Meg asked.

"I can't be sure," he shrugged. "But that was the age of dinosaurs, and I have heard that some evidence points to that possibility. The only other person to have seen it, as far as I know, was the high school teacher I showed it to. He didn't know anything, though. At least, he didn't say much. He did suggest that it was the remains of some animal that had been drowned in Noah's flood. That was about 1930, right after the Scopes monkey trial in Tennessee, and people generally were very leery about getting involved in anything hinting at evolution."

Carl was suddenly very thoughtful. "That seems reasonable," he mused. "Do you think so, Gramps? Maybe that is why the dinosaurs all disappeared."

"Except that Noah's flood was supposed to have happened on the other side of the world and sixty million years later," Gramps observed. "The creationists even like to claim that the flood covered the entire earth and that when it drained away it caused the Grand Canyon."

"That doesn't seem so unreasonable to me," Carl said. "Couldn't it have happened that way, Gramps?"

Gramps paused and rubbed his chin. "I suppose if there was a place for the water to drain into," he muttered slowly. "But the oceans would have already been full to the mountain heights! So where would the water go? And those caves in France where they are finding all of that cave art of the Cro-Magnon people couldn't have stayed dry enough to preserve what has survived for at least twenty thousand years. You think about that, Carl, and maybe you will want to know how the geologists explain the Grand Canyon. Now, let's go see if our dinosaur has disappeared again."

They drove along the fence as far as they could go and walked the remaining distance to the low canyon rim. Gramps hoisted the shovel he had taken from the truck onto his shoulder and observed, "I remember that I went down this grassy draw to where the cows had worn a trail to the trickle of water below. Then, I hiked up the narrow channel until I came to the red sandstone overlay. I hope I can still find it."

And he did. Little had changed except that the absence of grazing cattle, where once numerous farm herds once roamed, had permitted the narrow channel to become brush choked. Only a narrow path, kept open by secretive white tailed deer, allowed entrance. They stooped and twisted their way along the difficult trail until John stopped to examine the surroundings. The sandstone cliff rose on his right from a tangle of weeds and brush that had rooted into the gravelly soil. At various intervals, he paused to probe the vegetation and to push aside the concealing clutter. But his attention seemed riveted more on the red stone cliff. Suddenly he stopped and looked over his shoulder. "Eureka!" he shouted, "I have found it!"

He carefully pulled aside the tall horsetail weeds covering the cliff base and pointed to the initials etched head high into the soft sandstone. Almost eroded away by fifty years of wind and rain were the letters and date, JC–9/ 29/1930.

Awed by the place and date, Carl could only exclaim, "Gee, Gramps! What a treat this is!"

Meg's only comment was to wipe her sweating brow and moan, "Well, now I know why you waited so long to bring me here. What I wouldn't give for a tall, cold glass of ice tea!"

But John was unmindful of his wife's complaint. He was busy scraping away at the litter below and was immediately successful, for his shovel rasped differently in protest at an unyielding stony obstruction beneath the gravel. Several minutes later he stepped back and pointed down. Almost indistinguishable in its bed of gravel, was a bulky form, more log like than animal like. But, patiently, John moved away the surrounding shale and earth to reveal the contours of a femur-like fossilized bone of startling size.

"Wow," Carl breathed.

Meg quickly echoed her grandson. "Wow!" she exclaimed.

"Where is the rest of it?" Carl asked in wonderment.

"In the shale and gravel under the sandstone, I think," Gramps said, wiping his brow.

"Can't we dig it out?" Carl asked eagerly.

"Experienced paleontologists with a lot of help and equipment could—and a lot of time, too, I suppose. But this is not the kind of job for amateurs. Someday, the learned professors at some university might consider it, but this isn't an easy spot to get to or to excavate. It won't happen in my lifetime."

And Carl seemed to feel a clarification of purpose in his now wider world. *Maybe it will happen in mine,* he thought. That possibility was to be a signpost for him in the ensuing years.

Emotional shock does not go away quickly. It lingers on in the deep recesses of one's mind and only the changing times, new places, and new purposes can keep it at bay. John and Meg Claiborne knew that. The death of their only son and the ensuing separation from their grandson had been the most painful of all their life experiences. To continue living in Las Vegas could never have let them heal the hurt of losing those loved ones. In that respect, the return to John's roots and the subsequent building of their town with a multitude of new friends and interests had allowed them to heal. They had built scar tissue over their wounds and resumed living. Their grandson had been returned to them, and life became glorious again.

But when the tornado struck Carl's loved ones down, the grandparents wondered if they had the will and perseverance to go on living. One thing, though, remained in their favor. They understood that no human folly or evil could be blamed. Blind fate alone, devoid of malice, hate, vengeance, or betrayal, had destroyed Carl's family. That knowledge somehow diminished the shock and pain of the tragedy, and they could survive it. But the loss of the beloved grandson, as a secondary victim of the tornado, would be too painful. He was their only hereditary link with the future, and they rallied to save him. The days following their excursion into the canyon to view John's fossil discovery were to reveal the extent of their success. Carl Claiborne, too, would live to understand the reasons for the tragedy, and in the process, see his world through other windows.

At lunch that day, Carl was quietly thoughtful. His theory of the dinosaurs' extinction had been hasty and reasonable to him until Gramp's question about the water's need for a place to drain. And the idea that the whole world would necessarily have to be covered to the high mountains was preposterous. His thoughts then led him to reconsider the implausible story of Noah's Ark, impossibly large and cram-packed with hundreds or even thousands of pairs of animals to be fed and cared for by a small force of human survivors. *And for forty days and nights?* he mused. He shook his head and grunted.

"Gramps," he said, "I've been thinking about what you said about me going back to school. Do you suppose I could learn enough about dinosaurs to come back here some day and excavate that one in the canyon?"

Gramps, his reverie disrupted by the question, was shocked awake. For a long moment, he studied his grandson. His solemn face softened into a smile. "I don't doubt it in the least," he said. "When do you want to start?"

"This fall when the winter term begins, I think. I have to settle some things here about finances. And the church congregation needs to hear from me about my plans regarding their church."

"The church directors have been asking about that," Meg said, "and I told them that you would meet with them as soon as you felt like discussing it."

Carl's face grew solemn again, and he relapsed into a brooding silence. He swallowed, sniffed, and wiped away a tear. "I will be ready to meet with the whole congregation whenever the repairs to the church are completed. They deserve to hear my final message. It will not be a sermon but an announcement of my resignation as their pastor. What is to be done with the church building and grounds will be their decision." He looked at his grandfather and added, "—and the decision of the chief mortgage holders. Please tell them that, Grandmother."

"I will do that, Carl," Meg said. "The basic repairs are finished. In another week, the work should all be done. I will meet with the church board, and we will set a date."

Chapter 22

On Wednesday morning, June 18, four weeks after the tornado had struck, the repaired church opened its doors again to the people of Canadian County. But others outside the area who had been following the bizarre story of the tragedy also came, some out of curiosity, some uneasy and unsure of their own faith, and some professionally assigned by their media employers to get the news. During those four weeks, the story had been kept alive on talk-radio and television broadcasts, and the announcement of the meeting promised a climaxing finale. Earlier, an Oklahoma City television station had ask for an interview and been given permission to give coverage as a public service

"It will be on the evening news," its representative advised. "Will you object to our taping your sermon?"

Carl was quick to correct him. "It will not be a sermon," he said. "It will be more of a declaration of intent and a farewell address. And, no, I won't mind you taping it." He was silent for some moments as he stared wistfully out the big clear church windows. When he resumed again, his voice was grim. "Perhaps God will be watching and be informed of my suffering," he said sarcastically. "He certainly has not taken notice up to now. My message will outline my suspicions and how I hope to resolve them. It may or may not be newsworthy. Your programmers will have to decide that."

"Of course," his interviewers said.

Scheduled to begin at ten o'clock, Carl Claiborne's message to his former congregation was to attract more of an audience than he had anticipated. Meg and the church directors had wisely roped off the front half of available pews as a reserved area for regular church members. That area was quickly filled, and by ten o'clock no remaining seats remained in the entire church. Folding chairs were brought up from the basement and located in all but the wide center aisle. Some visitors were left standing in halls and doorways.

Meg and John, sitting near the center aisle, were astonished. "Maybe God doesn't care what has happened here," John murmured, "but the people of Oklahoma certainly do."

"Robert Haynes and his two daughters apparently do," Meg whispered. "They are three rows behind us. But I didn't see them come in. They must have come in the back way. I didn't expect them to be here after what Carl said took place in the El Reno parsonage the last time he was there."

"This may get a bit messy," John muttered. "The fundamentalists are the ones I worry about, and Robert Haynes is about as fundamental as they come. He may challenge Carl here as he did back in his parsonage."

"I had better let Carl know," Meg said.

She rose and made a last trip to the office sanctuary to warn Carl of the huge crowd he would be facing. "Why, Carl? Why have so many come?" she whispered.

"It doesn't matter, Grandmother," he soothed. "Whatever their reasons, I must speak my mind. But I may also be asking them to speak theirs. I am hoping for some revelation from them to help me understand what happened here four weeks ago."

"Your step-father and sisters are out there, too. I hope things don't get out of hand," Meg fretted.

"What do you mean, Grandmother? How could that happen?"

"I think there may be lot of people out there who, like your step-father, will not be agreeable to what you may have to say."

"I will not get drawn into matters of church doctrine, Grandmother. But I will speak my thoughts. And I do reserve the right to disagree if anyone out there persists in pushing his views too strongly. I may have had my faith weakened, but my ability to be diplomatic is still intact." He checked his watch. "It is time. Go out and join Gramps, and I will make my entrance as always."

He watched her go, picked up two books, and followed. The audience was hushed and immediately attentive. He walked quickly to the lectern near front center of the raised altar and lay aside the two books. He did not smile, for he had little joy in his heart. Solemnly, he acknowledged the mass of people, among who were the three remaining members of his immediate family. After a pretense of adjusting the height of the microphone, he took a deep breath and began. His words were slow and halting..

"Four weeks ago—" he sniffed, took a deep breath and began again. "Four weeks ago, this very morning—" He hesitated, looked away, and took another deep breath. "—in the dawn of a spring morning, I lost all that I held dearest in this world." Again he looked away, brushed at a tear-blurred eye and continued, his voice tremulous and quavering. "I lost my beloved mother, my devoted wife, and two beautiful children, one who—one who was not found for several days."

His listeners were silent as stones as his sorrow flowed outward to engulf them. He steadied himself and turned again to face the blur of forms, his jaws tight, his brow furrowed, his eyes narrowed. His delivery was very deliberate. By sheer will power, he forced himself onward.

"I know that you can imagine my pain," he quavered, "but not one of you can truly feel it! So, before you challenge what I will be saying, step into my shoes. I speak with the conviction and sincerity of one who has been deeply wounded. My pain is twofold, and I must explain why."

He paused as if to be sure of his words and began again. "I know of three kinds of human suffering: physical, mental, and spiritual. My loved ones — (sniff) — suffered the — (sniff) — the physical—pain of death. Those who found—their broken bodies—say that it was very short, and soon over. For that I can be grateful." Then, he paused again, a much longer pause, in which he stared through the big church windows, seeing with his mind's eye how it must have been that stormy morning when his grandfather and the rescue unit had found his family lying crushed and lifeless in the rubble.

"Their pain was quickly over," he repeated. "Mine continues. For me, it—it will never be over. It is both mental—and spiritual, and will be with me for as long as I live. Silent and invisible, it lies deep in my soul. Unless I can find some release from that pain, I have little reason to continue living." He hesitated and studied his audience. Had he been blind, the pews might have seemed empty, so silent were their rows of people. Only the muted whispers of the ceiling fans whirring in the early morning heat were any distraction at all. He looked up at them, sighed and lay his hands on one of the two books lying on the lectern. He lifted up the worn Bible for the hushed audience to see.

"This is the source of my spiritual pain," he said tearfully. "I have lived by this book. Until the morning of May 18, 1992, it served me well. Its teachings and words of promise shaped my life." He paused to look sorrowfully upward as he chewed his puckered lips. With stubborn determination, he continued, "I have known its contents. They are all so very familiar to me. But in these four weeks, they have failed to give me comfort or understanding. They have failed to tell me 'Why', and I have begun to doubt that they ever will."

His voice now held a trace of anger mixed with despair. The listeners in the filled pews heard his suggested condemnation, and he heard their responding gasps. Uneasily, they waited to hear more. More calmly, then, he moved from behind the lectern and took a step forward. A note of sarcasm crept into color a veiled accusation.

"I have heard ministers quote Its various passages concerning the many burdens that we as humans must sometimes carry," he said. "I have used them myself. 'God never places a greater burden on his followers than they can bear!' is a frequent platitude that I now find patently false. Sometimes despairing humans do indeed find their burdens too great. I have found it so, and I remember others who have found it so. I have known of their mental breakdowns. I have known of their suicides. Once, I believed that they were weak and that the fault was not God's but their weaknesses!" He paused again but did not turn away. "I was almost one of those," he confessed, his voice now strong and accusing. "The burden of my loss, with the awful revelation that my God had permitted the destruction of those whom he was supposed to love and watch over, were too much for me to bear. I felt as Christ on the cross must surely have felt when he cried out his suffering and despair, 'My God, My God, why hast thou forsaken me?'"

He turned and gazed reverently at the life-sized crucifix centered high up on the back wall. When he turned back again, he was apologetic. "I do not mean to liken my suffering to His," he said, "but those were my words in Nashville that morning when they brought the news to me of my loss. I am not sure that I can ever trust that God again."

His audience was no longer awe-stricken. It was shaken to the very foundation of its faith. He saw a flutter of facial tissues and handkerchiefs being brought hastily from purses and shirt pockets to cover stricken faces, and he heard muffled whimpers and sobs as the full implication of his words seeped in to probe the souls of his former parishioners.

His words were now gentle and sympathetic. "Feeling as I do," he said, "I can no longer serve as pastor of this church, or any church, until I can resolve my dilemma. I call on you for your understanding, and I request your counsel to help me know why I have been made to endure this great loss."

His voice raised, then, to indicate his impatience with past panacea offered to ease his misery. "But please do not burden me with platitudes! I have heard enough of those that promise revelation beyond the grave. And I have heard enough of those that plead for patience and trust, or those that say that God has his reasons and that we are not supposed to understand. Those are only excuses for our inability to comprehend the workings of a nebulous uncertain God! I am, now, made to wonder who and what that God really is. And I am made to question the wisdom of those ancients who were responsible for the teachings in this book."

He searched the stricken faces below him and waited. A multitude of emotions appeared there. Disappointment, fear, sorrow, dread, and an ugly anger mingled with pity, all were on the faces of those below him. Patiently, he waited for a scattered few to exit the building, their faces grim and unforgiving. For a long moment, he stared wistfully into the faces of his stepfather and two sisters. Robert Haynes' was anguished, his sisters' forsaken and sorrowful. Otherwise, they remained silent and inscrutable.

Slowly, he returned to his place behind the lectern. Laying the Bible to one side, he picked up the second book. As before, he stepped closer to the altar's edge and held it up. The audience stirred nervously and waited.

He had become calm. His voice was quiet and almost placid. It seemed almost as if the spiritual pain was suddenly eased and was being replaced by a new kind of strength. His aging grandparents understood, for they recognized the book being held up for the wondering audience to see. John lowered his lips close to Meg's ear and whispered softly, "Maybe he has already resolved his dilemma." She squeezed his arm gently and nodded.

"Two weeks ago, I discovered this book," he said. "It is an old college textbook which belonged to the father I was not blessed to know very well. He died when I was only five years old. This old textbook and other personal effects have been kept these many years by his parents, whom most of you know. They are my grandparents, John and Meg Claiborne, and they sit with you out there today. I want to acknowledge them now, for they alone rescued me from total despair and thoughts of suicide. They made me understand that it was not God who destroyed my family but the tornado. They made me see that God and Nature are not one and the same, and that God is often wrongly identified. I am hoping that this book will help me to understand what they have been saying. Its title is *Introductions to Historical Geology*. They have encouraged me to study it for clues to my confusion and despair.

"It is not a book recommended for young fundamentalist minds and for very good reasons," he explained. "It deals with the scientific views of creation that are contrary to religious teaching. In it, human history is based on evolutionary evidence, not divine creation principals. My own education was almost devoid of science, and I now want to learn why. I plan to enroll in a university for classes this fall. My intent is to measure the wisdom of modern wise men, who now are seeing our world through much larger windows than the ancients who gave us Judaism and Christianity a few thousand years ago. Their world was minuscule, their knowledge scanty, their window a mere peephole by comparison. I expect to learn much! Someday, I hope to return here to report my findings. I hope you will want to know what I have discovered."

He stepped back to the lectern and lay the old textbook atop the Bible. "I thank you for coming and sharing my thoughts," he said solemnly. "I know that they have been painful to you. They are even more painful for me. But please be reminded that we both came here voluntarily. Those who may be angry must remember that. They can air their dissent at the open meeting to be held immediately following this session. Those who are interested are invited to attend. My views are known. I shall not be present. Should anyone among you wish to speak with me privately, I will be available in the back office sanctuary from one o'clock to four o'clock this afternoon. I will be receptive to calm, rational discussions only." Then, he turned and walked slowly from the altar to the office sanctuary, leaving the numbed speechless people to ponder his words and their implications.

Chapter 23

Mavis Hobbs was visibly nervous. She had not expected to be faced with the task of fielding questions as controversial as the ones she feared might follow her ex-pastor's farewell address. But when she covertly studied the remaining group seated in the front half of the church pews, she saw mostly familiar faces. Though solemn and drawn, none appeared angry and combative. Even those of Robert Haynes and his daughters seemed sober and resigned.

She smoothed down a wisp of hair that had strayed from its assigned place and said quietly, "Before we begin the business part of our meeting, I want to ask for questions and comments concerning Reverend Claiborne's announcements. For my part, I have done as he suggested and stepped into his shoes. I greatly respect his sincerity and honesty. I cannot believe that I would feel differently under his tragic set of circumstances. He did not ask any one of us to subscribe to his new agenda. Our individual faiths are in our individual hands and should continue to be so. Anyone, who wants to ask questions or make comments should do so now."

Several hands went up. She recognized one and nodded. A grizzled ex-farmer, from the cotton country farther south, stood and squinted at those around him. "I have seen my share of hardships," he exclaimed. "I know how nature works. This old malarkey about the wrath of God is a bunch of you know what! I have had crops flattened by hail storms and my oldest son killed by lightening, and God had nothin' to do with it. I don't claim to know why. I just know, and no amount of prayin' would have made any difference. The preacher is right, and he deserves our support. And for whatever good it'll do, I say, 'God bless 'im!'" He sat down, grinning at the scattered applause which followed.

"I liked what he said about the wise men of today," a young woman said. "My husband is a high school science teacher who has very definite ideas about who and what we humans are, and he doesn't dare teach the science of evolution in depth for fear that the creationists will get him fired. I think that stinks, and the fact that my kids' education is being watered down by religious zealots who are in fear of losing their souls makes me furious. So I say, 'Welcome to the twenty-first century, Carl Claiborne!'"

It was then that Robert Haynes' hand shot up. He was recognized, and he rose red-faced and angry. John looked at Meg with raised brows. She shrugged, and whispered, "I am glad that Carl decided to be absent from this part of the meeting. He doesn't need an open fight with his step-father!"

"I hope he stays in his office," John muttered.

When Robert Haynes rose to speak, Naomi Haynes rose with him, her hand on his arm, her face tight and troubled. "No, Papa! Please don't," she pleaded. "If you make a scene, I will leave." Her younger sister joined her, and together they pulled him down. Angrily, he rose again, stalked through the scattering of chairs in the outer aisle, and exited through the back door. His two daughters, distraught and tearful, followed close behind. A scattering of others in the audience, their loyalties and their faiths in disarray, frowned their disapproval and silently departed the building.

Fewer hands were raised following their departure. But Mavis was determined to give audience to any and all who requested it. She nodded to a well-groomed gentleman who had only recently become a citizen of Chisholm. "You are new here," she said, "and we want to get acquainted. Would you like to introduce your self?"

"Of course," the man said, as he rose to stand. "I have met some of you, but I realize that I am a stranger to many. I am Percival Hargraves, a recently retired journalist from the Daily Oklahoman, and this is my wife, Dorothy." He paused for the murmurs of approval and light applause. "I have covered a number of assignments in this area in the past, and have watched the birth and growth of this wonderful little town. I decided it would be an ideal place to retire, and when we had a chance to buy a home here, my wife and I did. We think that we will like it and are eager to become active in the town's social and business affairs. This tragedy of your young pastor has been shocking to us, and we have watched its aftermath unfold daily. As a journalist, I find it a poignant human-interest story. As a fellow human being, I am made to wonder about how and why such a tragedy could happen. I think Carl Claiborne did very well in expressing his emotional confusion, and I get the feeling that we all suffer to a lesser degree with him. My question concerns what he meant by the phrase, and I quote, 'the ancient wise men's peephole on the world.'"

Mavis saw the knowing smile on John Claiborne face. "That question should be put to Carl," she said, "but in his absence perhaps his grandfather can give us some help with it."

John was thoughtful. He nodded and explained, "Carl was very close to destroying himself. I knew I had to dispel his notions of God having forsaken him. I usually do not interfere with a person's beliefs, but Carl needed help, and I knew that I had to get very basic. I expressed doubts about the identity of his God and the ability of the ancients to see and portray Him correctly. In my talks with Carl, I used that phrase, 'peep hole on the world', because the ancient people at that time had very limited knowledge of the real world. They must have been very confused about who and what they, as humans, really were. And I am convinced that their confusion has been passed down to our time." He hesitated and asked, "Do you want to hear more?"

There were raised brows and shrugs as his listeners turned to study their companions. "Of course," Percy Hargraves exclaimed. "I think I know what you are about to say, but I need to hear someone besides myself say it."

"Shoot!" a lady on the back row said loudly. "Those who don't like it can leave!" Others nodded.

"This may take a while," John warned. "I can best answer the whole question by talking to the entire group." He rose and took a place beside Mavis. She in turn took his vacated seat beside Meg.

"It may surprise you that a heretic of sort stands before you," he began "I have been in your presence many times and have seldom, if ever, expressed my religious beliefs. I have considered them personal as I have considered yours personal. But too many issues have come up this morning that need addressing. Too much smoke can hide a lot of small fires, and I would like to clear some of that smoke away.

"I believe that many human problems are caused by wrong decisions made from our failure to know ourselves as a species of evolving creatures. We want to believe that we are super beings who are deserving of special privileges because of a divine origin. The force identified as God is supposed to love us and protect us. When that God acts contrary to our expectations, the confusion and despair that it creates can be devastating. That happened to my grandson, Carl, who had only religious fundamentalism to solve his problem of rejection by his God. He could not rationalize the tragedy in a way that could rescue him from his terrible dilemma."

An older man in a back pew indicated his disapproval by leaning back and frowning. With arms folded tightly across his chest, he scowled and fretted. For several minutes, he continued to fidget and display signs of rising anger. Finally, when he could contain his displeasure no longer, he rose abruptly and blurted, "Mr. Claiborne, what makes you so sure that you know why God's actions need to be explained? Humans do not always need to know why He does what He does, and with all due respect to your grandson, it seems that he needs to learn a lesson in humility. Why doesn't he quit whining and just accept what God has given Him? What we don't need is some crackpot theory of evolution to make a lot of crazy explanations that are contrary to Scripture!"

John reddened. For some moments, he stood silent and unmoving. His steady gaze bore into the man's face. He chewed his lower lip for a moment, and said slowly, "Carl is not here to answer that question. But, in his talk this morning, he asked those who might disagree with him to step into his shoes and share his pain. Have you done that, Mr. Dunton? Have you ever experienced the trauma of having your entire family wiped out in a single instant? I have a faint remembrance of a bit of scripture from my child hood—and I cannot remember it exactly—but it said something about 'not going like the stolid ox to the slaughter' which indicates to me that we are supposed to question the reasons for things that happen to us. It certainly seems that any of us has the right and duty to question things that puzzle us. But, to put aside the awful tragedy that happened to young Carl Claiborne and to dismiss it as God's secret and needing no questioning, is absurd. That is the tactic of fundamentalists. They shrug off the questions that they cannot answer and call them God's dirty little secrets!"

Mr. Dunton was not appeased, nor had John meant him to be. Mr. Dunton was known to be very zealous in defending absolute truths in his religion, even though he did not always abide by them too closely himself.

"Mr. Claiborne!" he said scornfully, "You speak as the Devil's advocate! How can you presume to use some forgotten fragment of scripture to illustrate a point? You admit to being a heretic! Are you not also an atheist?"

John remained cool. His voice returned to its friendly conversational tone. "No," he said, "an atheist denies that there is a God. I just claim not to know who or what God is. Do you know, Mr. Dunton?"

"No, Mr. Claiborne, but I am willing to trust Scripture. It gives us a pretty good idea, and I'm satisfied to live by that."

"I am perfectly happy to let you believe that. Now, you should he willing to let me believe what I believe. I personally believe that religious fundamentalism can severely limit young minds that are kept closed tight against realities. One of the greatest thinkers of our time, Albert Einstein, recognized that. He said 'Religion without science is blind,' and I dare to paraphrase that bit of wisdom and say that science without religion has 20/20 vision.

"The Judo-Christian Bible was written by men who were without science. The essence of so much confusion today is that basic reality. They had almost no knowledge of the real world. They were totally unaware of the earth's size and shape or the great variety of life forms and ethnic people inhabiting its surface. They had no way of knowing about undiscovered continents, the cause of earthquakes, volcanoes, weather phenomena, microbes that cause disease, and a thousand other things that we take for granted in our world. Apparently, they did the very best they could to fit themselves into their mysterious part of the planet by inventing their own explanations."

Mr. Dunton waved away the awful accusations and interrupted loudly, "I don't want to hear anymore of that crap!"

"Mr. Hargraves asked to have an explanation for a phrase that Carl used this morning," John retorted. "You are not required to stay and listen."

"Humpf," Dunton snorted. He unceremoniously forced his way past those seated next to him and stalked from the building. Several other dismayed citizens of doubtful residency shook their heads to show their consternation and followed him out.

John Claiborne looked at Mavis and shrugged. "I should have known better than to be so blunt," he apologized. "I didn't mean to take up so much of your time."

A hand shot up and the question was asked again. "It seems that you must believe in evolution, then. Do you really not believe in the Christian God?"

"I believe that some power in the universe has caused it and us to be. But I am not arrogant enough to believe that humans can know everything. The concept of God may be knowable, but what God is, I believe is not knowable."

"Do you believe in Heaven and Hell?"

John smiled sardonically. "I have known people who deserved one or the other, but I have not known any who have gone to either place."

"And your grandson now has accepted your beliefs?"

"Only because his fundamentalist views failed him. His God failed him. His Bible failed him. He has come to see that the ancients created Genesis with nothing more than a small peep hole and their own fertile imaginations. Religious fundamentalists have believed it for centuries, and they are still touting it as the one and only explanation of the world and the humans in it. That is why they do all that they can to prevent scientific explanations from being taught in the public schools. They are exerting all kinds of pressure on school boards and teachers, and nothing is being done to oppose them. I think it is now time for rational people to stand up and take a stand for a new belief system based on hard evidence rather than imagination and supposition. But it will be difficult. Evolution is still unpopular. Human egos prefer to believe that humans have been divinely created. To admit their commonality with other life forms will hurt their tender egos.

"Many people do not know that a major struggle between the two belief systems will be waged here in the United States and the Western world in the next two or three generations. Carl now finds himself in the middle of that struggle because of circumstances he cannot deny. I think he will win. Thanks for listening. I am sorry that I upset Mr. Dunton and took so long."

"Don't be sorry," Percy Hargraves said. "I asked an honest question, and I got an honest answer. It's one that I can live with."

Mavis nervously refused to take any other comments. "We will begin the business portion of this meeting after a short break," she said. "Those who have no interest in these proceedings may leave now if they wish. Those who wish to be a part of the business meeting should be back here by eleven-thirty so that we can finish by lunch time."

Most of the assembly quietly exited. Some visited rest rooms or stepped outside for a bit of fresh air and to share their solemn thoughts with others. At least half of the original number returned to hear what was to be the new role of the church in the affairs of their community.

"I will keep it as informal as I can," Mavis said from her place before the front pews. "We need to begin thinking about the future of this church. Though many of our church members cannot be here for various reasons, we do need to begin airing our priorities. If we can just get a general feeling of what our members are thinking, we can take formal steps to implement whatever they decide to do at a later meeting. This has been a time of confusion for all of us. It will likely remain so for some time, and we need to discuss certain issues regarding finances, upkeep, and a continuance of services if that is the general consensus of the membership. Who cares to state an opinion first?"

Hands went up quickly through the scattering of people. And one by one, they were given time to speak and be heard. They expressed much regret and sorrow, and their nervousness, mingled with indecision and reticence, dragged the discussion through an ineffective half-hour. A mere handful was adamant that the church could survive its crisis, while an equal number admitted that they could not be comfortable in an environment so fraught with tragic memories. A straw vote indicated only continued indecision and reticence. Mavis looked at John and Meg who had remained silent and noncommittal.

"Perhaps, we should hear from John and Meg," she said. "After all, they are the chief stockholders. They donated the land and financed the final construction when the building was built seven years ago. The church has only paid that mortgage down to about ten thousand dollars. That might have some bearing on whether it will be viable to survive the loss of our key player. We all recognize that our pastor and his family were the pilots who steered this church and made it what it was. But it was also the elder Claibornes who made it possible for the church to be built. So, John, Meg, give us your thoughts."

Meg was immediately tearful. She wiped away a tear and took a deep breath. "It was not my church, or John's church, or Carl's church—it was Chisholm's church," she said adamantly. "A lot of good people poured their work and money into its construction. But it was first and foremost Carl's, in the sense that it was his dream and passion. But the tornado destroyed that. Now, I cannot feel the same as I once did. I could never have the same interest and enthusiasm. Let those who can, decide."

John gave his wife a quick embrace and nodded. "Meg is right," he said. "It was Chisholm's church and should remain as a Chisholm facility. Its function can be a variety of things. If not a church, it can be a Senior Center, or Community hall, or a library. My choice would be an institute for the furthering of tolerance and understanding between people."

Mavis nodded. "That sounds interesting, John. Can you enlarge on that?"

"I have no intention of deciding this issue," he declared, "but I am like Meg. I just cannot be very enthusiastic about this facility continuing as a church. It has been damaged not only in a physical sense but also in a psychological sense. Its steeple is gone, its stained glass windows are gone, its pastor and his family are gone. I could not be comfortable here in a church atmosphere again. But Chisholm and its citizens do need things other than the spiritual. I can think of no greater need than a beautiful hall where people can gather to hear quality programs to further our knowledge and understanding of the physical world. I believe that we already have a sufficient number of churches to take care of spiritual needs. The need now is to balance that agenda with one dedicated to logical and rational thought."

A hand immediately shot up from an older lady three pews back. "Yes, Mrs. Dimwitty?" Mavis said.

"Mr. Claiborne," the lady said sternly, "Just what kind of material would be included in those programs? Would they include religious programs?"

"I suppose they could, but as I have already said, churches of the county can and should supply that need."

"Then, Mr. Claiborne, you mean that you would have evolution and such garbage being openly advocated in a publicly owned facility?"

"Any thing of public interest might be on the agenda," John said patiently. "And there seems to be a great deal of interest in the sciences. Evolution as a science would certainly be there."

"Then I will never agree to your proposal, Mr. Claiborne!"

John squinted through his frown as he turned to face the opposition. "That is your right, Mrs. Dimwitty. You probably would not understand such programs anyway."

Quiet mirth and snickering followed, and Mavis, seeing the potential for antagonism more than decisive action, asked for a motion to close the discussion.

Chapter 24

Mrs. Dimwitty lost no time in going directly to the office sanctuary to speak her mind about the future use of the church building. She rapped on the closed door and waited. Carl laid aside the old geology text he had been reading and stepped to open it. Recognizing his visitor, he managed a faint smile and said, "Oh, please come in, Mrs. Dimwitty. What counsel can you give me about these tragic three weeks?"

"May I sit down?" she asked.

"Oh, please do," Carl said gesturing to the chair beside his desk where the geology textbook lay opened. The jaw bones of a chimpanzee lying along side others of early humans were graphically displayed. On the connecting page, the picture of a Neanderthal man gazed up as if to say, "I am a prehistoric man! Who are you?"

Mrs. Dimwitty took one look, drew back, and screeched, "Oh, God in Heaven! Spare me from this!" She quickly stepped to the open door and hastily exclaimed, "I'll come back another time."

"Please do," Carl said, smiling blandly. Closing the door behind her, he thought, *I hadn't realized the extent of some people's fears. A kind of paranoia rooted in superstition has taken over human minds to make them irrational! And I have been one of those!* He returned to study the pages of the textbook and saw only two printed white pages with illustrations to convey a meaning.

That's what all books are, he mused. *All books, including the Bible! Only the human minds that interpret the material in them are different!* He picked up the text and resumed his reading.

From time to time he found himself pausing to reconsider his message to the filled church that morning. It had been subject to a variety of interpretations also. What had been the thoughts of those who had listened? Doubts, regrets, and self-incrimination all crowded into his mind and clamored for a reassessment of his changing beliefs. He thought of his stepfather and two sisters who had sat silent and expressionless three pews behind his grandparents. Had they also been as fearful of his new beliefs? He had not been aware of his sisters' desperate opposition to their father's attempt to be heard in the later meeting, until the ringing telephone interrupted his reverie.

"Yes?" he said

It was Naomi, and her voice was agitated and tearful. "Carl," she said between sobs. "Ruth and I need to talk to you. We have just had a terrible fight with Papa. He is very angry about our behavior at the meeting this morning."

"Great Heavens, Naomi! What happened?"

"He was angry about something a lady said. When he rose to protest, we pulled him down and asked him not to make a scene. We were not supposed to be there anyway. It wasn't our meeting. Anyway, he stormed out and almost left us behind. And he has been mad and impossible ever since. Can you come over?"

Carl looked at his watch. "It's one thirty," he said. "I'll be there in a half hour." He hastily scrawled a note, hung it on the outside door, and hurried to his car. *Papa doesn't give up easily,* he thought.

He stopped to let his grandparents know where he was going and why. "Where is Gramps?" he asked.

"Down at the lake," Meg smiled. "When he gets uptight about things, he goes fishing. It's his therapy."

"I would join him if I could," Carl said ruefully, "but Naomi called. She was very upset and crying. Papa is being the Biblical patriarch. He senses that he is losing control, and for him that is a failure to do God's bidding. Mama could keep him in line when he got that way, but with her gone, I guess it's up to me."

"He seemed very angry when he stormed out of the meeting this morning," Meg said. "He may not want you to interfere. What will you do then?"

"I'll try to reason with him," Carl shrugged. "But he may order me to leave as he did when I was there that last time. My main concern now is to help my sisters with their problem. He still thinks of them as his children. They are really young adults who need understanding and love, not recrimination. It is going to be difficult for them."

Meg was thoughtful. Her dormant motherly instincts were stirring. "If this develops into a real crisis, they will be welcome here until things ease up. I really believe that your stepfather will do the best he can for everyone when he gets over the shock of these past weeks. He is going through a crisis, too, Carl."

"I know, Grandmother. I keep feeling the need to pray about it but find myself reluctant to do so. I just do not have faith in prayer anymore!"

"Perhaps prayer has its own kind of therapy, Carl. If it helps to ease a state of mind, it has its place, even if we cannot expect divine intervention."

Tearfully, he stepped to give her a hug and whispered, "Grandmother, you are so wise. If you were Catholic you would be eligible for sainthood!"

"I don't want to be a saint," she protested. "I just want everyone to be happy. You better go now and help your sisters."

"Yes," he sighed, "I had best be on my way."

He spent the thirty-minute drive to El Reno thinking about his boyhood years as a stepson to Robert Haynes. They had been good years, though strictly regimented by discipline and religious dogma. *I was the young tender sapling trained to grow and think in a certain way,* he thought. *What might I have been if my real father had lived to parent me?*

Then he recalled his mother's account of her own fatherless childhood in a household devoid of male figures. She, too, had been a tender young sapling trained to grow and think in a preset pattern not of her choosing. *We, and so many others, are what others have chosen for us to be, not what we ourselves might have chosen, had we had a different kind of guidance. Moses failed to include children in his Ten Commandments. He should have left out others of less importance and included, 'Honor thy children, for they are the future of mankind. Teach them wisdom above all things. Shape their will but do not break it!'*

"I like that," he chuckled. "Perhaps it will be useful if Papa remains too unyielding!"

He parked on the street near the church parsonage and surveyed it critically. The last time he had been there, he had been ordered to leave. Robert Haynes had exercised his patriarchal right, and removed his underling stepson from God's house that he had desecrated. He also had heard his stepson speak blasphemous words from the pulpit of the church in Chisholm. Then he had heard others in the later meeting, spouting evolutionary beliefs which he was not permitted to refute. *He has been sorely tested,* Carl mused. *Will he bar me from entering his house of God today?* He stepped from the car and walked casually to the front door.

Even before he had a chance to ring the bell, the door was opened. His stepfather stood looking severely from its shadows. "What does the heretic want at God's house," he asked.

"I have come to see my sisters," Carl said politely.

"You do not need to see your sisters," was the stern reply. "You will only confuse them more with your words of heresy. Why don't you just go back to your godless grandparents and leave us in peace? You have not been invited here."

"Naomi called and ask me to come. I consider that an invitation."

"I did, Papa," a voice said from behind him.

Papa stepped aside and said grudgingly, "Then talk with him outside this house. He is not welcome here."

Trembling and in tears, she stepped past her father and closed the door behind her. "Can we talk in the car?" she pleaded.

"Yes," Carl quavered. "I am so sorry. I have no right to put you in the middle of this."

As they got into the car, she sniffed and exclaimed, "It is not your fault. It's Papa's! He is so confused and so desperate. He has lost Mama, and now he is losing you. I think he is afraid of losing his own faith. Now, if he isn't careful, he is going to lose Ruth and me. I just do not know what to do!" She lost all control then and buried her head in her hands and wept. Carl cuddled her in his arms like he had the small sister in those times when she had been hurt by the death of a pet kitten or the loss of a childhood friend.

"You need to get away for a few days," he soothed. "Grandmother Claiborne said that you will be welcome there until we can resolve our problem with Papa."

"Can Ruth come, too?" she pleaded. "If Papa sees what he is doing to those he is supposed to love, maybe he will learn to be more tolerant and forgiving. Isn't that what religion is all about, Carl? Can't he see that?"

"Yes, Naomi, that's what it's all about. But sometimes we get lost in the wilderness of what is right and what is wrong and become combative and unreasonable. That is Papa's problem, and he needs to be told that. You wait here. I will force him to talk to me, and I will be heard even if it has to be on the street where the whole city can hear. You wait! I'll be back in a few minutes."

He strode purposefully back to the parsonage door and rang the bell. The door opened slowly to reveal his stepfather standing silently before him.

"Reverend Haynes," he said severely. "I challenge you to remember your Christian good sense and hear my advice to you. I speak to you not as a stepson but as the brother of two beautiful and loving children whose zealot of a father is in effect abandoning them to protect his own selfish ego. 'Honor thy father and thy mother' is a commandment no greater in importance than one that says, 'Honor thy children, for they are the future of mankind. Teach them wisdom, not bigotry, and shape their will, but break it not!' Does that make sense to you, Reverend Haynes? If it doesn't, then you will forever lose my respect and esteem for you and your childish Christian attitudes! And, more importantly, you will lose the love and respect of the only living members of the family left to you! Naomi asks that I take her and Ruth back with me to my grandparents' house where there is more love and warmth than here in this house of God."

He stepped back and beckoned for Naomi to join him. She came slowly up the walk, her whole manner a mute testimony of her dejection and sorrow. "If you and Ruth want to get clothing and personal effects for a few days at Grandmother's house, I'll wait," Carl said quietly.

She looked at her silent father and hesitated as he bowed his head and mouthed a wordless prayer. Slowly, he turned and disappeared into his sanctuary. A quiet and remorseful Ruth stepped forward and shook her head. "I don't want to go," she whimpered. "Papa will need me. I will stay here with him."

Naomi smiled wistfully and said. "Then I will stay, too," she said. "Maybe things will get better, and Papa will understand."

Carl nodded. "I think he will," he said. "Papa is not a bad person. He is also a victim of the tornado. It has hurt us all. But with open minds and clear thinking, we can get through these times. Please tell him that I love him." He felt better as he walked slowly back to his car.

Chapter 25

The next morning, Carl got a telephone call from Naomi. "Papa was very quiet this morning," she said. "I fixed him his favorite breakfast of ham, eggs, and pancakes."

"That's what Mama used to fixed him when he was out of sorts," Carl replied.

"I know. Maybe, it wasn't a good idea. When he sat down to eat, he didn't say grace. He just buried his head in his hands and wept. But he ate everything on his plate and complimented me on my cooking. 'It was just like your mama's,' he said. Then, he broke down and cried again."

"Did he say anything?"

"When I was gathering up the dishes, he put his arm around me and wept silently. Then he said, 'I have been so lost without your mother!' Of course, I wept with him, and when Ruth came in later, we all huddled together and cried."

"And now you have me crying," Carl blubbered.

"I am sorry, Carl, but I think that he needs to go through a crisis. He has not been willing to question God's purpose in all of this for fear that he will be considered irreverent."

"I know. I was on the verge of destroying myself. I needed a new perspective. Papa needs one, too. What can we do, Naomi?"

"Be patient with him. When Ruth told him what you said yesterday about loving him, he secluded himself in his room. Later, I went to check on him, and he showed me what you had said about a commandment for children. He had written it down, and he plans to use it as a theme for his sermon next Sunday. I think that you should plan on coming."

"What if it is slanted and negative, Naomi?"

"It won't be, Carl. He is too remorseful. I think he is moving toward a more reasonable way of thinking. He did say that perhaps he should be looking through wider windows. I suspect that he is softening his views somewhat."

"I hope so," Carl said."

"And, Carl, please come to church Sunday!"

"Maybe I will," he said.

"And, Carl, could I borrow that old textbook of your father's? I want to see what all our good Baptists are so concerned about."

"And what will Papa think about that, Naomi?"

"Maybe he will want to read it, too," Naomi mused.

"I wouldn't bet on it," Carl said.

The following Saturday, the local El Reno paper carried its usual calendar of church affairs and Sunday services. Among them was the Hosanna Baptist Church's statement that its regular minister would be delivering the sermon after a month's absence. "Reverend Haynes has been in mourning since the death of his wife, daughter-in-law, and two grandchildren in the tornado which struck the town of Chisholm, May 18th. We continue our condolence and prayers for him and his remaining family. Welcome back, Reverend Haynes."

Meg, as usual, read the announcement and mentioned it to her husband. "I think we should go," she said.

John disagreed. "I doubt that we would be warmly received after him hearing my little speech at our church meeting last Tuesday. I think he may be a bit hostile. After all, I did label myself as a heretic, and he never got a chance to denounce my views. My presence there would be like rubbing salt into an open wound."

"I hope Carl will go."

"He may not be looked on with much favor, either. His views are now too much like mine. And I know who he will blame for that!"

"Don't be too hard on yourself, John. Carl was headed straight toward suicide. You know that, and he knows it, too!"

"Humans make too much of a big deal about their beliefs. I did, and now I wish I had kept my mouth shut. In some people's eyes, I am now a bogie man to be thought of as Satan's right hand. And I am still the same person I've always been."

Meg smiled wistfully. "Yes," she said, "the same big teddy bear, but with a label, 'Beware! Heretic Inside!'"

They heard the door open and footsteps in the hall. "Carl, can you come in here for a minute?" Meg called.

"What's up?" he said, as he picked a burr from his trousers. "I walked a mile up and down the river and did some thinking."

"Good!" John exclaimed. "That's just what this world needs, more thinkers! Your grandmother has something for you to read. Then you may have something else to think about."

She handed him the opened section of newspaper. "Your stepfather will be back in the pulpit tomorrow," she said.

He scanned it quickly. "Yes, I know," he said. "Naomi told me over the phone. That's what I have been thinking about. I guess I'll go and hear him. I had almost decided to skip it. Then, it struck me that maybe he might be seeing through other windows, too. If he is, he will need some encouragement."

"I want to go," Meg said.

"Good! Naomi is hoping you will. She said that he is building his sermon around something I said to him on Wednesday. That worries me some, because it might be either positive or negative. But if Naomi is so upbeat about it, I will go. How about Gramps?" He looked searchingly at the older man and waited.

John shrugged and pondered the question. He squinted out the window and finally said, "I told your Grandmother that I doubt I'll be welcome after speaking my mind the other day, and nothing makes me feel so uncomfortable as being in a place where I'm not wanted."

"I have known few churches to ever regard anyone as unwelcome," Carl said. "Besides, the discomfort you may feel will be yours alone. The worst Papa can do is to turn up the heat a little if he decides to pontificate. I would really like for you to go, Gramps. And Naomi told me to urge you to come."

Gramps chuckled softly. "Then, I will go!" he declared. "Call Naomi and tell her that we will be there, and that your grandmother

Meg and I invite her, Ruth, and their father to a special family dinner at El Reno's finest dining facility, the old Highway 66 Palace. We will make reservations for 1:30 Sunday if they are free to accept. Will that be okay with you, Meg?"

"Oh, it is wonderful, John. Maybe I can think of something to make it really special! And, Carl, be sure that they accept so we can confirm the reservation."

For a moment, Carl's old hurts threatened to over power him again. The word, 'family', was like a hot iron in his brain. He trembled and stifled a sob. Swallowing hard, he nodded and said, "I will do that, Grandmother."

John and Meg were more curious than nervous when they entered the Hosanna Baptist Church on Sunday morning. Carl was neither. He preferred to be optimistic. Naomi had successfully eased his concern that her father might deliver a stormy sermon of condemnation to those who dared to question Baptist orthodoxy. And her father's gracious acceptance of the dinner invitation seemed to imply that he would moderate is Sunday message. *But if he doesn't,* he thought, *I will sit serenely through it with my sisters, as a duck might sit through a rain storm.*

He joined them in their usual place where they whispered solemnly and quietly about their father's changing attitudes. The grandparents were ushered to seats near the center aisles. There, they sat, relaxed and meditative, through the choir's opening hymns.

When the usual announcements, prayers, and offerings, were attended to, the young assistant minister stood behind the lectern and expressed continued sympathy and condolences to those who had been in mourning for loved ones lost to the tornado a month earlier. "One of those," he said, "is our own most beloved and respected minister, Reverend Robert Haynes. He has had a very confused and trying time, but he tells me that he can now see some hope in the aftermath of that tragedy. His sermon this morning will be about Wisdom, Past and Present. Please stand and give Reverend Haynes a warm welcome back!"

The spirited applause and murmurs of approval, mixed with sniffles and tears, warmed and assured the middle-aged man as he stepped to take his place behind the lectern. He placed his Bible and notes on the lectern top and wiped his eyes with a tissue. Patiently, he waited for the applause to wane and for the congregation to be seated again. Even John and Meg were almost overwhelmed by the outpouring of emotion. They stole quick looks at Carl and his two sisters sitting on a front pew, their heads bowed, their arms trying to embrace each other.

"I thank you so much for your display of love and loyalty," Reverend Haynes said. "It is such love and kindness that helps to heal our hurts. I am made to remember a phrase from my high school English class, 'the balm of hurt minds'! And in the past weeks, my mind and the minds of those close to me, have indeed been sorely hurt. And tentacles of that hurt have reached into the minds of our friends and brethren in this church community, into our lovely city, and throughout our county. Part of that hurt has been because of our inability to understand the reasons behind this tragedy. Even now, we continue to struggle as we seek understanding.

"Faced with that dilemma, I have sought much counsel, most of which has proved unreal and questionable. Then, when I was despairing most, I found help in quite an unusual place. It came surprisingly from my own children. Though they are no longer babes, I find much meaning in a bit of scripture from Psalms 8: 2 that I quote for you this morning: 'Out of the mouths of babes and sucklings hast thou ordained strength because of thine enemies.' From the mouths of my children, I have found strength and wisdom to defeat two terrible enemies, confusion and despair. For it is they who have stood resolute against those enemies with their own wisdom and understanding.

"I resisted that wisdom and understanding at first. I was the Biblical patriarch who had the right and duty to do that. I renounced their efforts to void my anger against those who would have opinions other than my own. Their wisdom and understanding I considered inconsequential and contrary to scripture. For that pomposity, I now ask them to forgive me. And I ask all in this congregation to forgive me for using this personal event in my family affairs as a part of the message I bring to you this morning.

"To be sure that you will understand my new perspective, I want to quote a very wise and appropriate line that I heard recently. It is not from scripture, though it may seem to be. That line I quote now: 'The commandment to honor thy father and thy mother is no greater or less than one that says, 'Honor thy children, for they are the future of mankind. Teach them wisdom, not bigotry, and shape their will but break it not!'" He paused for a long moment as if to let the words soak into the minds of his congregation. Then he repeated it again, slowly and with quiet emphasis. Again he paused and turned his attention to his three adult children sitting below him. He smiled and began again.

"That was an admonition to me by my very dear stepson, Carl, whom you all know," he said.

He beckoned to those on the front row and quavered, "Would you please come up here, Carl, and accept my gratitude for such a wonderful bit of wisdom?"

They embraced there on the altar and wept unashamedly as they whispered words of regret and hope. The congregation, hushed and tearful, stood again in thoughtful silence. Carl returned to his pew, nodded to the hushed congregation, and sat down. The standing mass of people also sat and soberly waited.

"Those words, spoken by my stepson, have triggered a host of revelations to me," the pastor continued. "'Teach them wisdom,' he said. And I was made to wonder about that word, 'wisdom'! How is wisdom to be taught? Surely the teacher of wisdom must be wise if he is to teach others wisdom. And I wondered about my wisdom and the wisdom of ancient times! What were the wise old men's notions about wisdom being taught? Who were they trying to teach?

"I found this in Proverbs 4: 7. 'Wisdom is the principle thing: therefore, get wisdom: and with all thy getting, get understanding.' Ah, what a jewel of wisdom that is!" he exclaimed. Looking long and hard at his congregation, he repeated, "—and with all thy getting, get understanding!'" He nodded as if to imprint his next statement on every mind in his congregation "Surely, that is what wisdom is all about!"

He stepped to the front of the lectern and stared silently over the heads of the people below him. He squinted at the stained glass windows, looked up at the vaulted ceiling, and down again to fix his stern gaze on the congregation, "Our tragedy of six weeks ago requires, above all, wisdom and understanding!" he emphasized. Again, after a short pause, he said deliberately and emphatically, "—but not the wisdom of the ancients. Not the wisdom of Abraham! Not the wisdom of Moses and the many prophets who followed him! They could not know about tornadoes. They could not know about air masses that come together to create destructive storms. They could not understand that Nature has its own set of rules, and that those rules have no consideration for humans who may get in Nature's way.

"Only our wise men of today have that kind of wisdom. We humans must learn to share their understanding and to respect those rules. Nature does not hear prayers. Nature cares nothing about our puny human needs or feelings!" He paused as if to be sure he was choosing his own best words of wisdom. They became conciliatory.

"It is becoming plain to me that we should be giving more attention to the wise men of today than to the wise men of two and three thousand years ago. Today's wisdom is remarkable, and we would not dare choose ancient medical practices over the medical technology of today. Nor would we grow and prepare our food based on the wisdom of that time. Now, I am made to wonder why we should rely so much on ancient wisdom to explain weather phenomena like tornadoes and lightening storms. It is time to quit blaming God for the natural tragedies like the one that took our family. Perhaps, if God is really angry with his human children, it is because of our tendency to blame him for natural disasters. We should, instead, be reading modern books of wisdom as well as the Bible. And we should be listening to the professors in the universities and colleges in this great land who understand such wisdom! And we should stop being suspicious of their teachings. They surely have greater truths than we have been willing to acknowledge, and we should be very careful about picking and choosing wisdom just to suit our past concepts.

"For clarification of that statement, I will paraphrase another bit of wisdom, not from the present, but from St. Matthew, chapter 22, verse 21. These are Jesus' words to the Pharisees, who came to him seeking counsel as to whom they owed their allegiance. 'Render therefore unto Caesar the things that are Caesar's, and unto God the things that are God's.' Jesus said." The pastor hesitated and took a deep breath as if to assess the mood of his congregation.

His eyes swept over the many rows of pews and saw none of the customary drowsers and catnappers. All faces were turned toward him as if his words were going to wipe out mysteries that had remained too long unsolved. He vigorously thumped his opened Bible and repeated the verse from St. Matthew. "Render unto Caesar those things that are Caesar's," he admonished sternly, "and unto God those things that are God's!"

A long pause permitted the meaning of his words to trickle into cautious minds. Some heads nodded perceptibly as if to give him encouragement. Then he drove in the nail to clinch his argument. "In the same way," he said, leaning forward, "I believe that we must render unto the ancient wise men the wisdom that was theirs at that time, and unto the wise men of today the wisdom which is theirs at this moment!

"Wisdom is not of the past alone!" he cautioned. "Wisdom is not an exclusive commodity of the ancient wise men! Wisdom is and has forever been a quality and quantity subject to revision. Through time, a flat earth of unknown size has become a round world of known size. A sun that was thought to move around the flat earth of unknown size has become a sun that is the center of our solar system. That round world, as we now know it, moves around that sun!"

Again he drew back and waited, alternating his gaze so that it rested momentarily on his opened Bible, only to be lifted again to flit here and there over his congregation. "The ancients, my dear parishioners," he finally admitted very solemnly, "were not so wise after all. Perhaps their concept of God was right for them at the time, but is it right for our modern world? Is He really a God of great love and, at the same time, a capricious, petulant God capable of great anger and violence?" Pause. "Did he permit, for some unknown reason, the deaths of four innocent, gentle, and loving people who had been his devoted followers?" Pause. "Or is this God a less personal God who is not as concerned with the humans who inhabit his earth as we have been led to believe?" Pause. "That is a question that now troubles me.

"In closing, I leave you with these thoughts," he said. "I shall be pondering them in the months and years ahead. I hope you will give them serious consideration. Let me restate those lines from Proverbs. 'Wisdom is the principal thing: therefore get wisdom; and with all thy getting, get understanding!'" He closed his Bible and lay it upon the lectern. With a tinge of weariness in his voice, he said humbly, "I ask now for our assistant pastor to give the closing prayer." But despite his apparent weariness, his whole manner seemed to radiate confidence as he stepped aside to relinquish his place behind the lectern.

The closing prayer was short and to the point. "Thank thee, O Lord, for this message. Help us to understand Thy purpose. Give us strength to seek wisdom and understanding. In Thy name we ask, O Lord, Amen."

Robert Haynes then walked quietly down the center aisle, and, as if to offer reassurance to those whose fragile faiths may have been weakened by their pastor's sermon, the organist played the hymn, *How Great Thou Art.* As he had often done in the past, he stationed himself at the door to shake the hands and give his blessing to the departing worshipers. On this day he hoped to assess the effect of his unusual message on their hearts and minds. Knowing that his reference to their God's ambiguity was not what they were accustomed to hearing, he expected to be challenged. He was not, however, and was gratified to hear only positive comments.

"A great sermon!" one man said. "It made a great deal of sense. I hope we can hear more wisdom and less rhetoric in the future!"

"Your description of the wisdom of those old Biblical guys was an eye opener!" another remarked. "It's no wonder that they were so quick to blame all the bad stuff on God. I hope others think so, too!"

"Well," one elderly lady said, " I have often wondered how God could be so good one minute and so cruel the next. Maybe, like you said, if he is mad at the human race, it's because of the way we've been accusing him of stuff he doesn't do!"

"I don't know, Reverend," an old man said, "but you might oughta be a bit more careful. Some of these folks aren't gonna buy your new notions about God not bein' personal and watchin' our every move. You may be hearin' from them about the time you expect be rehired."

"I'll keep that in mind," the pastor chuckled. When the last one had gone, he closed up the big doors and joined his family for Sunday dinner at The Route 66 Palace.

Chapter 26

The Route 66 Palace Hotel was a place of times past. Built in 1928 in anticipation of continuing prosperity and the completion of a new cross country highway, it had a long and colorful history. It had survived depression, drought, dust storms and the unfortunate migration of many middle Americans on the magic road west to Golden California. But it had not opened its doors to that horde, for the cost of its services for one night easily exceeded the ordinary citizen's weekly income. Its clientele, in those pre-war years, had been the more visible and affluent travelers eager to get from west to east or east to west. Screen darlings and swashbuckling heroes from Hollywood needing to go east, took the road that would get them there quickest and with the least discomfort. The Palace became known as an oasis in the middle of a land threatened with drought and depression. Built at the intersection of two important highways, it had prospered.

But, as for all things designed for a specific period in history, the changing times had not been kind to it. As air travel disrupted the flow of affluent motorists and Interstate 40 siphoned off the overnight travelers, its reputation as a special place to mingle with the elite and famous had not kept it afloat. It closed its doors and waited. "Change or die!" its business consultants warned. New owners recognized its obsolescence. Their only hope was to convert its use to include middle class folk who could appreciate its elegance. The budget-wise and ordinary working Joe's had money to spend if they could be catered to at a cost they could afford. The answer was to offer good food to be served in an atmosphere of elegance.

A number of rooms closest to the main dining hall were converted into private dining rooms to be reserved for small family dinners. To enhance their appeal, they were given names of former famous personages who were known to have been overnight guest of the Palace Hotel. The strategy worked. People came from all over central Oklahoma to enjoy the good food and elegance, and to fantasize their presence in the same spots that Hedy Lamar, Joan Crawford, Henry Fonda, John Steinback, and a host of others had once occupied. When she received Naomi's telephone call the previous Saturday accepting the Sunday dinner invitation, Meg Claiborne had reserved the Gary Cooper Room.

"Why?" John had asked. "Why Gary Cooper?"

"Because he has always reminded me of you," she said.

"I'm flattered, but be honest, Meg! You had a crush on him when you were young, didn't you?"

"Yes, I did," she admitted, "but he was unavailable, and you were my second choice."

"Well, being second choice to Gary Cooper is better that being second choice to Harpo or Chico Marx," John said.

"There is another reason," Meg said.

"Oh?"

"Do you remember the scene in the movie, *Sergeant York*, where his mother expressed her confusion about the workings of God?"

"I'm not sure. Tell me."

Meg squinted up her face as if to better recall that bit of lost trivia. She looked skyward and said, "'The Lord certainly works in mysterious ways!' and Sergeant York said, 'He sure do, Maw!' Or something liks that. And all I have heard these past four weeks has been a variation of that theme. Now, I have decided to steer our guest's minds down other roads with Gary Cooper's picture looking on. They won't know about the Gary Cooper thing, but I will. I need the illusion to help me do it better."

Her husband had screwed up his face and expressed his doubts. "Gee, Meg," he had said. "I don't understand. Should I ask?"

"Don't ask!" she had replied tartly. "I will work it out!"

And John hadn't asked. He had absolute faith in his wife's good sense and perception about social affairs. When Sunday arrived and

Carl and his Haynes family were shown to the Gary Cooper room, John accepted a place at the end of the carefully set table and waited.

The small family group of six people, still basking in the glow of Robert Hayne's sermon, was affable. Its sorrows had been temporarily set aside in anticipation of an event that promised good food and fellowship.

Meg quickly established herself as hostess and from her place beside John rose and said, "John and I are so grateful for this occasion. It is almost as if our mysterious God has arranged for us to meet here today for a surcease of our past sorrows so that we might begin anew. I have asked our head-waiter to serve a family style dinner in the old tradition of American families. I need to feel that we are now a family, brought together by unusual circumstances. I want each of you to join me in that dream. Only in that sense can we look to the future with hope and new enthusiasm.

"I have also asked that, before our dinner is served, we be given a few minutes to consider quietly our options for the future. I know it is traditional for people of faith to offer a moment of grace before eating. I want to honor that tradition, but in a different way. I would like for each of us to do it silently with special thoughts about his or her future. My purpose in doing that is to help us to turn away from the sad past and to anticipate the dawning of a brighter tomorrow. Afterwards, if anyone cares to share those thoughts, I think they might be useful in helping others to seek new wisdom for the future. Let each of us now take five minutes to do a bit of soul searching."

Five minutes can be a long time for idle thoughts to filter out, but for minds turning away from sorrow to contemplate new agendas, five minutes can pass quickly. For the young whose dreams have been suddenly and rudely interrupted, five minutes can be a time for clearing the debris of disaster away and tidying up the mental landscape.

For John, whose dreams had been mostly realized, five minutes were more than enough, and he sat back and covertly studied those with their closed eyes and solemn faces as they pondered the roads to be taken. *They are so vulnerable,* he thought. *And the two ministers are perhaps the most vulnerable of all. They are like creatures that must shed their cocoons before beginning new unexpected roles. I wonder if they will share their thoughts with us.*

Meg, too, was soon open-eyed and attentive. She looked at her husband and smiled. He saw her misty eyes and knew that her thoughts had not been on her agenda but on the needs of those others around her. That was Meg's way. As Carl had said, she was deserving of sainthood!

One by one the others roused themselves from their five minutes of introspection. Every single one wore smiles, some wistful, some thoughtful, some faint. Robert Haynes' was carefully masked and uncertain.

"My psychology professor had us do this little exercise when I was a young college girl," Meg explained. "It has been my way of praying. In place of asking, I make wishes for the things I would like most. Then I set a course to make them happen. Most of the time it works for me. When it doesn't, I study the failure and begin again."

Carl nodded his head and said, "I have only recently learned that from Grandmother. It forces one to be humble and stubborn at the same time.

"I recently discovered among my father's things an old worn book of poetry. In it, I have found a great deal of wisdom from the wise men of the past few hundred years. One bit of verse that stuck in my mind was titled 'Invictus'. I'm not sure what that means but I think it has something to do with being invincible. It's by a man named William Henley, and I recommend it to be read by anyone who feels lost and hopeless. It has given me new insights into who I am, and I expect to use its message in the future when I begin my new search for knowledge. I have visions of a college career in which I can seek the wisdom my stepfather has talked about. Someday, I hope to share that wisdom with young minds that are lost and searching for enlightenment. Perhaps, I can begin in Chisholm with an institute to be located in the remodeled church—an institute named in honor of my grandparents. That is my dream. That is my prayer."

"I will pray for that, too, Carl," Meg said. She looked at Robert

Haynes and asked, "Does Reverend Haynes want to add anything to that?"

"If that is Carl's dream, I will add my prayers to help make it a reality," he said. "I will also continue to thank God for the revelations I have been privileged to experience in these past few days. My hope is that I might share them with others who are also looking for wisdom and understanding. That will be my new mission."

Meg turned her gaze back to John. "We haven't heard from you, John. What are your thoughts?" she asked.

"Carl's dream will be my dream," he said. "I have visions of a small but high quality college facility in our town of Chisholm dedicated to an understanding of the earth sciences. It can start on the present grounds where the church now stands. When Carl returns to us from his studies in five or six years, perhaps the Claiborne Institute of Earth Sciences will become a reality. When it is time for me and my dear wife to depart this earth, whatever earthly assets remain to us, we will dedicate to the Institute. If Meg agrees, I mean!"

Meg immediately puckered up and whimpered, "Oh, John, how wonderful! Of course I agree!" Then, in an attempt to turn the attention away from her tears, she looked at the two young sisters who had remained silent. She nodded when Ruth, almost timidly, raised her hand.

"I don't quite know how to say this, Mrs. Claiborne," she said, "but in my five minutes of prayer, I included you, and I wished that you would be my honorary grandmother. Both my other grandmothers are dead — and with my mother—" She paused and wept. Meg quickly went to her and knelt to cuddle her.

"I am so happy to be your grandmother," she quavered. "I have never had a granddaughter! Oh, how I will love and cherish you! And we will learn what your dreams are, and we will make them come true."

Tearful and pleading, Naomi immediately knelt with them and sobbed, "I'm eighteen and I feel so much alone! Am I too old to be your granddaughter?"

Meg caressed her hair. "Oh, no, no, no!" she cried. She looked at

John and whimpered, "I'm being adopted, John! I had not counted on this to be one of the blessings of this wonderful day." Then she laughed through her tears and exclaimed to her two new granddaughters, "But there is one condition! You must adopt my husband, too!"

And in that moment, John became a grandfather for the second and third times. He wiped away a tear and turned toward his wife. In his best Gary Cooper drawl, he said, "The Lord shorely do work in mysterious ways!"

"Yes, He shorley do!" Meg said.

Standing with them, Reverend Haynes, with his arms trying to enfold them all, looked heavenward and exulted, "Praise God! The healing has begun! I pray that it will continue!"

"Amen," John exclaimed. "Bring on the food!"

* * * * * * * * The End * * * * * * * *

Conclusion

In the fall of 1992, Carl Claiborne enrolled in the Redlands Community College at El Reno. Entrance tests at two different universities revealed serious weaknesses in mathematics and the physical sciences, and his only recourse was to take classes to correct those deficiencies. Intelligent and highly motivated, he successfully completed courses in algebra, geometry, trigonometry, physics, chemistry, and ancient history in the fall and winter terms.

He easily passed subsequent entrance tests, and the following spring he was accepted by the University of Colorado for undergraduate work in the earth sciences. He finished the requirements for a Bachelor of Science degree in three years and advanced degrees two years later. Part of his advanced degree work was spent working with geologists and paleontologists in the fossil rich states west of the Rocky Mountains.

Even his crowded schedules did not prevent him from making short visits to Chisholm where he was booked as a guest speaker in forums and seminars at the fledgling Claiborne Institute. His two sisters, awed by his accomplishments, became so interested in his work that they followed his lead and earned their own degrees in the earth sciences. In 1999, when the Claiborne Institute became a reality, Naomi, the older one, became part of its new faculty of ten able professors. Ruth later married and accepted a position as a science teacher in a large Denver high school.

Their father eventually left the ministry at the behest of the Baptist Church hierarchy who had become unhappy and impatient with his enlightened views. He later became the Institute's head fund-raiser and financial advisor. His prayers for the continued healing of his family had been realized.

At this writing, the chief benefactors, Meg and John Claiborne, now in their mid eighties, relax in their comfortable home where they can look out and see the elite body of two hundred students hurrying to meet class schedules in the campus' five main buildings.

Sometimes they walk there, too, when the weather is nice and they want to be reminded of what the Institute means. The sign over the main entrance says it well:

A TRUE UNIVERSITY OF THESE DAYS IS A COLLECTION OF INQUIRING MINDS

And sometimes, they just want to feel a part of the dream that sprouted and grew out of the rubble of a tragic storm. Reserved for them on a memorial site where the church parsonage once stood is a plot where they have asked to be buried.

They go there sometimes to talk and remember the night of the tornado. But the lingering sorrow for the innocent victims of that early morning storm in 1992 is mellowed now by the good things that have followed it. And sometimes Meg will hold him in a close embrace, shake her head solemnly, and in her best hill country drawl say, "The Lord shorely do work in mysterious ways!"

And in his easy Gary Cooper manner, John replies, "He shorley do, Ma! He shorely do!"

* *